The Little Red (Sox) Book

CURSE REVERSED EDITION

A Revisionist Red Sox History

Bill Lee

with Jim Prime

TRIUMPH
B O O K S
CHICAGO

Images on pages 70 and 137 courtesy of AP/Wide World Photos. Images on pages 58, 62, 69, and 86 courtesy of CORBIS/Bettman. All other images created by alteration; source photo credits as follows. Page xvi: Mao Tse-tung image courtesy of AP/Wide World Pho-tos, Bill Lee image courtesy of Bill Lee. Page xix: Pope John Paul II and Bud Selig images courtesy of AP/Wide World Photos. Page 47: Einstein image courtesy of AP/Wide World Photos, Bill Lee image courtesy of Bill Lee. Page 63: Babe Ruth and Ted Williams image courtesy of AP/Wide World Photos. Page 72: Robert McNamara and Ted Williams images courtesy of AP/Wide World Photos. Page 76: Moe Berg image courtesy of Corbis/Bettman, background image from James Bond film courtesy of MGM Studios. Page 89: Nazi general and Fenway Park images courtesy of AP/Wide World Photos. Page 121: Jackie Robinson and Ted Williams images courtesy of AP/Wide World Photos. Page 138: Jackie Robinson and John F. Kennedy images courtesy of AP/Wide World Photos. Page 177: Bucky Dent and Lib-erace images courtesy of AP/Wide World Photos. Page 192: Hall of Fame plaque image courtesy of AP/Wide World Photos, Bill Lee image courtesy of Bill Lee.

Library of Congress Cataloging-in-Publication Data for hardcover edition

Lee, Bill, 1946–
    The little Red (Sox) book : a revisionist Red Sox history / Bill Lee with Jim Prime.
        p. cm.
    Includes bibliographical references.
    ISBN 1-57243-527-5 (hc)
        1. Boston Red Sox (Baseball team)—Anecdotes. 2. Boston Red Sox (Baseball team)—Humor. I. Prime, Jim. II. Title.

GV875.B62 L44 2003
796.357'64'0974461—dc21

                                        2002072139

Printed in the United States of America
ISBN 1-57243-731-6
Interior design by Patricia Frey

Contents

Foreword to the
Curse Reversed Edition

*"You're welcome, Red Sox fans! But beware the
'Curse of the Spaceman.'"*

—Bill Lee

fter 86 years the Boston Red Sox are once again world champions, and everyone in New England seems to be taking a little piece of the credit for our change in luck. I don't want to rain on anyone's parade, but this *Little Red (Sox) Book* that you're holding is the *real* reason the curse was reversed. As I accurately predicted, it has served as "the amulet for our reversal of fortunes." Wow, sometimes I even amaze myself. Yes, it was I who reversed the curse, with a little assistance from my coauthor, Jim Prime.

The two of us wrote a book that included various altered bits of Red Sox history—from the nonsale of Babe Ruth to the Yankees, to Ted Williams killing Adolf Hitler with a line drive, to the integration of baseball with Jackie Robinson opting for Boston and not Brooklyn. It's true that we didn't write anything as fantastic as the corny Hollywood script the 2004 team followed. I mean, who would believe that Jesus would be in center field; that the entire team would be sipping Jack Daniels before the most important games of their careers; that the Red Sox would stage the greatest comeback in baseball history after being down three games to none to our friends, the New York Yankees; or that the last game of the World Series would come complete with a lunar eclipse? You can't make that stuff up and still maintain your credibility as a writer.

I was the one who unleashed the concept of "the curse of the Bambino," when I explained the idea to an attentive Dan Shaughnessey, the *Boston Globe* columnist who wrote a book about it and then became rich and famous (check please, Dan). It is now only fitting that I am the one to have rid the Red Sox Nation of this accursed curse.

I don't expect praise in my lifetime. I do know that God is now on our side and that it will not be another 86 years before Aunt Hilda from Lowell is once again throwing up on her shoes after drinking too many celebratory Sam Adams.

Unless . . .

I don't want to cause any trouble or distress for the Red Sox Nation now that the curse of the Bambino has been KO'd (you're welcome once again, Red Sox fans), but I do require certain assurances or I will be forced to create a *new* curse. This time it will be the "Curse of the Spaceman." Think about it: they sold the Babe to the Yankees for $100,000, but they traded me, another legendary Boston southpaw, to Montreal for Stan Papi. I ask you: who should be more pissed off at the Red Sox? If something isn't done, there will be books about it and movies, and someday a Red Sox pitcher will want to dig me up and drill me in the ass with a pitch.

How can you avoid the "Curse of the Spaceman"? There are just a few small things that will ensure championship teams in Beantown for years to come:

1. An invitation to a keg party at Theo Epstein's place to watch tapes of the seventh game of the ALCS.

2. An acknowledgment of my blacklisting from the majors and a written apology from Bud Selig on behalf of Major League Baseball.

3. A prominent feature at Fenway to be named after me, as in "Pesky's Pole" or "Williamsburg." I suggest "Lee's Latrine."

4. "Special brownies" to be available in the staff and media dining room, and to fans on certain holidays.

5. A guarantee that my number will never be retired, but instead will always be kept active, passed down from generation to generation.

6. An orthopedic MRI machine at Massachusetts General Hospital—to be endowed by Graig Nettles.

7. A new rule forbidding any Red Sox player from taking part in major league competition on my birthday (December 28).

It all seems little enough to ask to avoid another 86 years of misery, wouldn't you say?

—Bill Lee, March 2005

Preface to the First Edition

*"Dogma is less useful than cow dung. One
can make whatever
one likes out of it, even revisionism."*
—Chairman Mao Tse-tung,
from an interview with Andre Malraux, 1965

"My karma ran over my dogma."
—Chairman Bill Lee, from a message seen
spray-painted on a California minibus, circa 1968

When people call me a left-winger they aren't just talking about my pitching arm. I am the only leftist southpaw ever to play in the American League. After we lost the 1975 World Series to the Cincinnati Reds, I went to Red China. Mao Tse-tung was still alive at that point, and I attended Chou En-Lai's three-day funeral, although I played snooker at the Peace Hotel through most of it. While I was there I saw the real Big Red Machine and let me tell you, Cincinnati's version pales in comparison. I travel regularly to Cuba, and I believe that it should become our 51st state, if only because we need more Luis Tiants and Tony Olivas in the game. I was the first ballplayer to play in Red China, communist Cuba, and Reagan's "Evil Empire," the former Soviet Union. In short, I am part baseball Bolshevik and part armchair anarchist. Baseball is without borders and I believe that ballplayers should be too.

Don't get me wrong; as many great leftist Americans before me have stated: "I am not now, nor have I ever been, a member of the Communist Party." That statement was generally made in response to questions from Senator Joe McCarthy, not to be confused with former Red Sox manager Joe McCarthy, who was a much more tolerant and open-minded man. The baseball establishment has called me a pinko-commie-fag, but actually I am a baseball conservative. I'm a baseball player and a subsistence farmer. I don't believe in profit making, and the only law I totally believe in is the law of gravity.

> "Outside of a dog, a book is man's best friend.
> Inside of a dog, it is too dark to read."
> —Groucho Marx

Despite opinions to the contrary from guys like Don Zimmer and the late Billy Martin, I am not the "Red Menace" that threatens American values; I'm more like Dennis the Menace, and the baseball establishment is my Mister Wilson.

> "I am not a Marxist."
> —Karl Marx

I adhere to the principles of the Quechua Indians of the "high" Andes (pun intended). They share everything. I am a socially liberal, hippie, Rastafarian, Zen Buddhist communist with a lot of Catholic guilt. Admittedly, I am trying to dissolve the nation. My philosophy knows no borders because the Earth is round, a one-celled organism. I don't believe in the word *sovereignty*. In that respect, I am an anarchist, and when I ran for president my promise was that once elected, I would choose not to serve. That was my entire platform.

I am not a subversive. The closest I ever came to being part of a Gang of Four was when Ferguson Jenkins, Rick Wise, Bernie Carbo, Jim Willoughby, and I formed the Gang of Five, otherwise known as the Loyal Order of the Buffalo Heads. As a Marxist-Leninist, I tend to be as much influenced by Groucho (Marx) and

John (Lennon) as by Karl (Marx) and Vladimir Ilyich (Lenin). Philosophically, I am equal parts Maharishi Mahesh Yogi and Yogi Berra. My life view has been forged by the logical humanism of Buckminster Fuller, tempered with the illogical home run of Bucky Dent.

I *am* calling for a revolution, though. Not that I want to replace Tiananmen Square with Kenmore Square and stand in front of a tank (although I have been tanked in Kenmore Square on several occasions, once in a burgundy Rolls Royce with Derek Sanderson). No, there are already enough revolting people in baseball—George Steinbrenner and Graig Nettles, to name but two. (Few people know that Nettles was toilet trained at gunpoint.) Nor am I looking to start a class struggle. The people in baseball with any class are struggling enough these days. The revolution that I am seeking is a revolution of thought. I am trying to enlist a Red (Sox) Guard, a Red (Sox) Army, not to weed out independent thought but to cultivate it, as Henry David Thoreau did. Thoreau said in *Walden*: "If a man does not keep pace with his companions, perhaps it is because he hears a different drummer. Let him step to the music which he hears, however measured or far away." In baseball's great parade, everyone else seems to be marching to John Philip Sousa while I am keeping pace with the distant sound of a kazoo. I am asking you to ignore the march and saunter along with me.

My precise political affiliation is with the Rhinoceros Party, an ideology that embraces actual, true conservatism. Our motto is "We are not sheep. We will not follow." Among other things, our platform states:

> "Chinese dissident Liu Gang, 34, was arrested in Liaoyuan and charged with failing to honor a previous court order that required him to report to the police periodically to inform them of his latest thoughts."
>
> —report in
> *News of the World*

- No guns, no butter. They'll both kill you.
- Tear down all de-fences.

Why did I write this book? Well, aside from the fact that they locked me in a small room and put a hot light on me, I wrote this book to (a) enlighten the masses about the real menaces facing baseball, and (b) offer hope and solace to Red Sox fans by revising Red Sox history.

> "This is a tough park for a hitter when the air-conditioning is blowing in."
>
> —Bob Boone describing the Houston Astrodome

Believe it or not, baseball's biggest threat does not come from disparity, expansion, contraction, rabbit balls, corked bats, or even performance-enhancing drugs. The real menaces are clichés and false conservatism, i.e., tampering with the purity* of baseball. (*See German purity laws governing beer; you can put only natural ingredients in there.) The enemies of baseball are the bourgeois reactionaries who are trampling on the game by creating designated hitters, artificial turf, aluminum bats, domed stadiums, furry mascots, luxury boxes—all the stuff that doesn't belong in a ballpark. The game stands up very well on its own, thank you very much. Charlie Finley and others wanted to eliminate jobs and specialize. Specialization breeds extinction—and major league baseball is close to the endangered species list. The game is inherently good. It's the people who run it who are threatening to destroy it.

As for Red Sox history, I equate the trials and tribulations of the Sox to a girl named Abigail Williams, a character created by playwright Arthur Miller in *The Crucible*. (Miller later married Marilyn Monroe after she had put her spell on Yankee Joe DiMaggio.) Abigail basically turned state's evidence on a bunch of people, claiming that they were witches. And all the prelates and church people used this claim as an excuse to steal their property. The true and hearty souls from New England were persecuted by the wealthy through the guise of religion, and Abigail Williams was the symbol of this abuse. It's a sad truth that people believe a good-looking liar before they believe a hard-working farmer. They are swayed by that actress—that seductive Lucrezia Borgia character—and become enthralled with her. She uses her power to steal this guy's farm and that guy's rich bottomland. And then she calls her victims witches and the men burn them at the stake, hang them from the cross, and steal property from their kids. The Red Sox came into New England and inherited that persona, that mystique of Abigail Williams.

Red Sox owner Harry Frazee basically accused Babe Ruth of the mortal sin of enjoying life and sent him to New York to burn. Like many others before and after him, Ruth was "banned in Boston." He took a bite of Boston's forbidden fruit and his punishment

> "The good people sleep much better at night than the bad people. Of course, the bad people enjoy the waking hours much more."
> —Woody Allen

was banishment to the Big Apple, which is rotten to the core. The Red Sox gathered some great players, and then all of a sudden they were all sent to New York—away from Fenway's Garden of Eden to New York's nether regions, into the marketplace for 30 pieces of silver. They were spirited away, so we lost all the good players, not just Ruth. Looking back at it, it's almost spooky. Poof! There goes Ruth. Presto! Good-bye Sparky Lyle. Abracadabra, Luis Tiant is wearing a Yankees uniform. Zap! Good-bye Mr. Boggs. Zoom! Rocket Roger lands in New York. No wonder the Red Sox have never stood a chance!

Sure, we should have played better at times, and sometimes we have deserved our fate. But why does the ball take a tricky hop and go through Buckner's legs? Why does Freddie Lynn crash into the wall in Game 6? Why does Jim Rice's wrist get broken in 1975? Why couldn't Zimmer get along with pitchers? What if he didn't have

> "Get rid of the designated hitter. Get rid of Astroturf. Revamp old ballparks. Outlaw mascots. Outlaw video replays."
> —Chairman Lee

those three steel plates in his head from being beaned—by a pitcher? Why does Zimmer pull all kinds of stunts—like benching me in 1978—and then resurface as bench coach for one of the great modern dynasties of the New York Yankees? What if Lansdowne Street had gone out 10 more feet so that the Wall had been a little farther away? Or what if there was no Wall at all? Bucky Dent's home run wouldn't have gone out in any other ballpark except Fenway. Why do all these things seem to befall the Red Sox?

My *Little Red (Sox) Book* attempts to answer these questions and alter Red Sox history. Despite the fiction, it is mostly a book of truth. It attempts to show Red Sox fans the nirvana they could have had but for a few large missteps. If nothing else, this book will lift the Red Sox nation to a higher level of consciousness. Read this book quickly. Read it carefully. Read it often. It just might be the amulet for our reversal of fortune.

—**Bill Lee**

What Bothers the Spaceman?
By Mono Puff

Far from the crowd
He's the day-watchman
Walk past the trees
He used to swing from
What bothers the spaceman?
The teeth in his head
I'm sure he could smile for us
Wave to the people
Out on the lawn
Mr. Ellis and Mr. Lee
Mr. Lee and me
What bothers the spaceman?
What's left for him now?
I'm sure he could smile for us
Lee lee lee lee lee lee lee lee
Lee lee lee lee lee lee lee lee
Lee lee lee lee lee lee lee

Acknowledgments

Thanks to Bill Nowlin, Diana, Richard MacKinnon, John Hildebrand, Gerry Hoare, Linda Cann, Tom Bast, Blythe Hurley, Bilal Dardai, Kris Anstrats, and Ben Robicheau.

Introduction

"I always understood everything Casey Stengel said, which sometimes worried me. But I know that all my hours with Casey helped prepare me for Billy Lee."
—Lee's former USC coach, Rod Dedeaux

"Do not fear to be eccentric in opinion, for every opinion now accepted was once eccentric."
—Bertrand Russell

"History is a pack of lies about events that never happened told by people who weren't there."
—George Santayana

Between books and bats, the Boston Red Sox represent an environmentalist's worst nightmare. Louisville Sluggers aside, several small forests have been destroyed to produce the extraordinary number of books written about the Boston Red Sox and their star-crossed history. The story of Babe Ruth's sale to the New York Yankees alone—and the resultant "curse of the Bambino"—has helped defoliate several acres of northern Maine woodland. But Red Sox history is somewhat akin to New England weather: everybody complains about it but nobody does anything to change it. Well, this book changes Red Sox history. We make no apologies for that. We didn't like the way it turned out, so we changed it. We'll leave it to others to try to change the weather.

Neither Bill Lee nor I were history majors. We had to look most of this stuff up, and doubtless we still got some of it wrong. Sometimes we changed actual historical events from one year to another (we moved up Jimmie Foxx's arrival in Boston by a few years, for example; we also brought Tris Speaker home from Cleveland and moved the Green Monster to right field) but since we decided to change it anyway, who cares?

During the late sixties, *Quotations from Chairman Mao*, better known as "Mao's Little Red Book," was among the most widely read and famous books on Earth. The book consisted of the collected thoughts and observations of Chinese Communist Party chairman Mao Tse-tung and was meant to be a guide for daily living and the

Mao Tse-tung and Bill Lee: a summit between two noted lefties.

furtherance of the cultural revolution. Mao encouraged the youth of China to attack the bourgeois sectors of Chinese society. Everyone carried the book and was encouraged to use it as a weapon to effect change. Mao's quotations were repeated, examined, and applied throughout communist China.

Bill Lee's Little Red Book is the philosophical opposite of Mao's. Where Mao discouraged and penalized "incorrect" or independent thinking, Chairman Lee encourages it. Where Mao forbade Western music, Lee looks to it as a conduit for independent thought and action.

The "what if" segments of this book are meant to be pure fantasy, a pleasing primer for hot stove leaguers who like to imagine what would have happened if the Red Sox had not been cursed with the loss of the Bambino and other man-made and natural calamities. In order to demonstrate the huge impact each individual change would have on the Red Sox (and the world), each chapter reverts back to "reality" as we know it and departs from that point.

Please note that these fantasies are not meant to diminish in any way the pioneering and courageous efforts of owners such as Branch Rickey, whose enlightened actions led to the integration of baseball. In addition, there is not a major league player with whom I have ever spoken—including Ted Williams—who saw his service to his country during World War II as anything less than an honor. Ted told me many times that he did not regret those years in any way, shape, or form.

In addition, the big changes presented also require a number of smaller changes to support them. The "fact" that Babe Ruth never left Boston and Harry Frazee was replaced as owner by Joe Kennedy leads us to abort the systematic dismantling of the Red Sox initiated by Frazee. Likewise, Jackie Robinson's arrival in Boston necessitates other changes in the Red Sox lineup.

Many people probably imagine Lee and me writing this book in an Outer Mongolian yurt, while snorting rosin bags newly arrived from Haiti. Not so. Lee's yurt is in Vermont. (It isn't really a yurt; it's a farm in Craftsbury, a town whose website offers the following admonition: "This is a basic geographic reference, intended to show relative location of adjacent towns. Directional accuracy is limited to 16 compass points. There isn't even the slightest suggestion that one can necessarily travel directly from one town to the next, as in 'You can't get there from here.'" Obviously this is Lee's kind of existentialist town.) And his drug of choice these days is not rosin but Advil, which he refers to in these pages as a "reprieve from death."

Sports Illustrated once referred to Bill Lee as "America's paragon of left-handedness." Not only is he left-handed, he is also left-wing and decidedly left out of baseball's mainstream. He has strong opinions and doesn't mind expressing them in no uncertain terms. He also has a wicked, often bizarre sense of humor, and no one is safe from his biting wit, not even Lee himself.

If there is only one thing you need to know about Bill Lee, it is that he loves baseball. That is not just a cliché. Bill Lee's love of baseball is real and passionate, and sometimes unrequited. Lee loves everything about the game, at least on the field. He savors it the way some men savor a fine cigar. He loves the smells of the game, the sights of the game, the sounds of the game, the personalities of the game. He loves the purity of the game and worries about those who would sully it. He would play it for nothing—and usually does. He is fortunate that his university major was geography because his pursuit of baseball has caused him to cover a lot of ground in recent years. A recent tour of western Canada took him to such baseball meccas as Fin Flon, Medicine Hat, Slave Lake, Swift Current, Peace River, Vermillion, Kamloops, and High Level. "Thank God places like this exist," he says.

Bill Lee's *Little Red (Sox) Book* reflects Lee's Zen-Buddhist ("with a touch of Catholic guilt"), hippie philosophies and provides him a virtually unfettered vehicle to explore anything and everything having to do with the Red Sox in particular and baseball in general—not to mention his occasional forays into areas and subjects that have little to do with baseball at all. Only Bill Lee has the credibility to integrate yoga, Yogi,

> "No one can earn a million dollars honestly."
> —William Jennings Bryan

Yoda, breathing techniques, visualization, several Eastern philosophies, and global warming into playing baseball.

Lee may not be a historian, but his credentials as a philosopher are very much in order. Aside from his overriding theory that the Earth is a hanging slider with God coming to the plate, he has philosophies on almost everything pertaining to baseball and life. He quotes Ouspensky, Gurdjieff, Nietzsche, Vonnegut, and Buckminster Fuller. And then he quotes George Scott, Mickey Rivers, Oil Can Boyd, and Bernie Carbo. And then back to Descartes, followed by a bit of Eckersley, Machiavelli followed by Petrocelli, and so on . . .

He believes that baseball must be saved from itself, like the spoiled and insolent child it has become. "Bud Selig is what Mao would have called a 'tofu tiger'—he has no teeth. The commissioner is a puppet of the owners, and that causes resentment within the players' union," he asserts. "Fans are the ones who support the franchises and they're paying the players' salaries. As a socialist, I see only one solution. They have to storm the commissioner's office as the peasants stormed the Bastille during the French Revolution. They have to take control. I will lead the mob." Lee feels that baseball is the bellwether of society, and if baseball is sick, so is society. "Ralph Nader had it right: sports, and not religion, is now the opiate of the masses. We have to shake ourselves out of that opiate-induced state and return the game to what it used to be: a pastime, not a religion under Pope Bud Selig. We succeeded in saving Fenway Park, now we have to start a campaign to save baseball." Lee's former teammate Tom House once summed up Bill Lee's relationship with baseball's

Bud Selig announcing his new ideas for the destruction of baseball.

establishment: "Bill realized very early the ludicrousness of being in a position where so many intellectual vegetables have so much authority and influence over the way he lives his life."[1]

The idea for Bill Lee's *Little Red (Sox) Book* was mine, and I take full credit or blame for it. Lee embraced the idea immediately and ran with it as only he can. Being a very intelligent and eclectic man, the Spaceman has an excellent perspective on the world of baseball, especially the Red Sox. If anyone has the imagination, background, and incentive, to alter the fate of the Red Sox, it is surely Chairman Lee, who personally suffered some of the slings and arrows of their outrageous fortune.

They say that in war the winners get to write the history books. Well, not this time. This time the loser gets the final say. Call it fiction if you like. We prefer the term *revisionism*. Not historical fiction but fictional history. It just sounds more important somehow. You can even call it "hysterics" if you are so inclined. Napoleon said, "History is a lie agreed upon." In any case, the Yankees have been benefiting from revisionism for years. How else could you justify Joe Gordon winning the MVP in 1942 instead of Triple Crown winner Ted Williams? Williams led the American League in average with .356, RBIs with 137, and homers with 36. Gordon led the league in only two categories that season: strikeouts and errors by second basemen. New York writers changed history by making him the MVP of the American League. Now *that's* revisionism of Forrest Gumpian proportions. The previous year those same writers decided that a 56-game hitting streak was more important than a .406 batting average, when that's like comparing a circus sideshow to the main event. Unfortunately for Ted, baseball's Big Top has always been the Big Apple.

Ever read a history book and wish you didn't know the ending in advance? Well, dear reader, you've come to the right place. Assuming that you are a Red Sox fan, this history book has a happy ending—lots of happy endings, actually. There is a fine

> "The historian should be fearless and incorruptible; a man of independence, loving frankness and truth; one who, as the poet says, calls a fig a fig and a spade a spade. He should yield to neither hatred nor affection, nor should he be unsparing and unpitying. He should be neither shy nor deprecating, but an impartial judge, giving each side all it deserves but no more. He should know in his writing no country and no city; he should bow to no authority and acknowledge no king. He should never consider what this or that man will think, but should state the facts as they really occurred."
>
> —Lucian, A.D. 120–200

line between baseball fact and fiction anyway; and sometimes, like the chalk lines that mark the base paths, it gets blurred. Robert Redford borrowed heavily from Ted Williams' storybook career when he portrayed Roy Hobbs in *The Natural*. And yet whose life story was more fantastic and dramatic: Hobbs' or Williams'? I'd pick the flesh and blood Williams over the celluloid Hobbs every time. And Kevin Costner, in *Field of Dreams*, revised reality to resurrect an entire baseball team in the cornfields of Iowa.

My point is: where does reality stop and revisionism begin? This book is based on fact. It is not an outright lie. Most things here are possible. Very few have been invented entirely from our imagination. Maybe some. OK, OK, a lot of this book is outright lies, the kind of stuff your mother would have washed your mouth out for uttering within her earshot.

All rookie ballplayers dream of making baseball history. Brash young Ted Williams was even specific about how he would accomplish it, saying, "After I retire, I want to walk down the street and have people say, 'There goes the greatest hitter who ever lived!'" Then he went out and made it happen. With the publication of the *Little Red (Sox) Book*, Lee has achieved a double play of sorts. He was a significant part of Red Sox history, and now he has literally rewritten Red Sox history. If it catches on, generations hence—when those mutated survivors emerge from the debris of the Bomb—they may discover a copy and not be able to distinguish reality from revision. Bill and I would like that. As Heywood Broun observed: "Posterity is as likely to be wrong as anybody else."

Lee also provides the reader with a primer on baseball and the Red Sox. In addition to rewriting Red Sox history, Lee offers up his unique views on today's game and the game of yesteryear. He skewers selfish ballplayers, self-satisfied owners, and bastardized baseball. The Spaceman has a unique view of baseball and the world in general. He is not now and never will be enshrined in the Hall of Fame in Cooperstown, or even in the

Red Sox Hall of Fame—although he should be—but he *is* enshrined in the Baseball Reliquary's Shrine of the Eternals, in California. Fittingly, the Baseball Reliquary is "a nonprofit, educational organization dedicated to fostering an appreciation of American art and culture through the context of baseball history. . . . Similar in concept to the National Baseball Hall of Fame, the Shrine of the Eternals differs philosophically in that statistical accomplishment is not the sole criterion for election; rather, candidates are nominated based on overall contributions to, and impact made on, baseball." Only three individuals each year are so honored. Lee now shares membership with other baseball iconoclasts, including Moe Berg, Jim Bouton, Dock Ellis, Curt Flood, Satchel Paige, Jimmy Piersall, Pam Postema, Bill Veeck Jr., Minnie Minoso, Mark Fidrych, and Shoeless Joe Jackson. By anyone's standards, that is a dream team for the ages—and a team that would give the baseball establishment nightmares.

A self-confessed Bolshevik-anarchist, Lee is as contradictory as that label implies. He is actually a baseball conservative in his desire to see the game return to its roots and traditions. Paradoxically, in today's buttoned-down baseball world, that makes him a flaming radical. Chairman Lee's baseball manifesto is packed with wisdom. It will have you nodding your head in agreement or shaking your head in disbelief.

—Jim Prime

CHAPTER 1

Chairman Lee's Baseball Manifesto

*"What baseball needs is a benevolent
dictator, elected by the fans.
I, Chairman Lee, am offering to
take on the job."*

—Chairman Lee

I was kind of the Alice in Wonderland of the game. Like Alice, I had to pass through the looking glass every time I walked to the pitcher's mound. My proudest accomplishment as a baseball player was to prove once and for all that you can exist and prosper—at least for a while—as a dual personality in baseball. As a person and a citizen, I made every effort to protect and defend Mother Earth, and I couldn't care less about earning more than the other guy or having a better job than the guy next door. That kind of soul-destroying competition doesn't interest me. But when I was pitching, I morphed into an entirely different person. I am a driven, extremely competitive being and I am out to win. Early Wynn was like that. Batters never dared to dig in on him or they'd get a fastball near their chin. Once he was asked if he would throw at his own mother. His reply? "Only if she was really crowding the plate."

> "When we lost I couldn't sleep at night. When we win I can't sleep at night. But when you win, you wake up feeling better."
>
> —Joe Torre

That competitive nature becomes something of a paradox for me now, since I often pitch for both teams in charity games. I always get the "W" and the "L" in the same game. It opens a bunch of philosophical questions about my yin and yang, sort of like Casey Stengel's observation that "Good pitching will beat good hitting every time; and vice versa." Or his other comment: "Most ballgames are lost, not won." The trouble is, I understand exactly what he means!

> "One pill makes you larger
> And one pill makes you small,
> And the ones that mother
>   gives you
> Don't do anything at all.
> Go ask Alice
> When she's 10 feet tall."
>
> —from the song "White Rabbit" by Jefferson Airplane

My problems arose when my off-field persona—the real me—clashed with the mentality of major league baseball. I was not going to back down from my fundamental beliefs for the sake of some inane, nonsensical sound bite. I decided that early on. I am a living, thinking person, and I was not going to pander to the lowest common denominator. I had to stand up for my beliefs. To sit idly by and let injustice flourish would have compromised me as a human being and as a pitcher. That's why I am proud that I was able to maintain my compassion while retaining my competitive edge. I go on junkets to Cuba, and the competition is amazing and exhilarating, but so is being able to give a little Cuban boy his first pair of shoes.

I know that I was able to entertain the fans with my pitching skills—and maybe with a well-placed comment here and there. Baseball isn't brain surgery; it's meant to be enjoyed. As I said in my first book, *The Wrong Stuff*, I want to be remembered as someone with a social conscience, a man who cares about the planet and is a champion of the little guy—but also a guy who would take you out in a heartbeat if the game was on the line.

It is entirely consistent and fitting that I was kicked out of baseball and blacklisted for sticking up for my fellow ballplayers. I stuck up for Bernie Carbo while I was with the Red Sox and I was sent to Montreal for Stan Papi; then I stuck up for Rodney Scott in Montreal and I was kicked out of baseball. This is baseball's version of McCarthyism. It's almost better to be kicked out of a false conservative fraternity like that than to be part of it and, by staying in, condone their actions. You are probably thinking: You can't be a conservative and a lefty at the same time (look what happened to Dravecky—his arm fell off). My answer to that is simple: Since the earth is round, I'm so far left, I'm right. That's right, sports fans: *Bill Lee is a baseball conservative!* I am conservative about the integrity and the traditions of the game. Pure baseball is without politics. That's why a staunch Republican like Ted Williams got along so well with a Bolshevik like me. The Splinter and the Spaceman are both baseball conservatives.

But that doesn't mean baseball has to be a conservative, boring game. Baseball needs more color and fewer clichés. In today's game, the purpose is to sell, and to do that you apparently have to live by clichés and political correctness. There are too many millionaire ballplayers. Money is like cow shit: it's best when spread around. Today's ballplayers all sound like that old *Saturday Night Live* routine with their "Baseball's been berry berry good to me" rhetoric. Baseball freethinkers such as the Buffalo Heads, like their namesake beast of the Great Plains, are threatened with extinction in today's bland-leading-the-bland environment.

Baseball is a utopian world because it has no timeline and should have no boundaries. That's why domed stadiums are sacrilegious. Playing under a dome is like playing in an old pair of

> "Man may penetrate the outer reaches of the universe, he may solve the very secret of eternity itself, but for me, the ultimate experience is to witness the flawless execution of the hit-and-run."
>
> —Branch Rickey

sneakers. The baseball is a metaphor for the earth, and in reality I have always been more of an Earthman than a Spaceman.

I believe that strikeouts are as fascist as Benito Mussolini. Fastballs rise up the ladder. Good morning Reggie, good afternoon Reggie, and good night Reggie! Curveballs are very organic and very natural. They make optimum use of gravity. They induce ground balls. Ground balls are what I attempted to achieve because they stimulate and incorporate so many more aspects of the game. The hitter has to hit it, the fielder has to catch and throw it, and the first baseman has to field it. It leads to double plays, and double plays are as democratic as the U.S. Congress, because everyone gets involved (although Congress makes far more errors). The so-called Leephus pitch employed gravity to its maximum potential, with batters trying to hit the perfect unhittable pitch going straight down. Forget the apple falling on his head; Isaac Newton could have used that pitch to illustrate the concept of gravity. A change-up is like the four seasons. First the hitter experiences the promise of spring, then the anticipation of summer, then the reality of autumn. Then, all of a sudden he's frozen like it's the dead of winter, and he grounds out weakly to the shortstop. He ages a full year in one at-bat.

> "Duct tape is like the Force. It has a light side, a dark side, and it holds the universe together."
>
> —Carl Zwanzig

My first edict as commissioner of baseball will be to disintegrate the designated hitter, annihilate the Astroturf, doom the domes, and massacre the mascots. Pitchers will be allowed to hit—or at least try—and guys like Roger Clemens won't have carte blanche to throw at people. All of a sudden, he'll be just another .500 fascist fastball pitcher.

> "Life is like a baseball game. When you think a fastball is coming, you've got to be ready to hit the curve."
>
> —Jaja Q

I'll maintain smaller ballparks. I'll outlaw video replays. I'll eliminate interleague play. The World Series will be played only in daytime. I'll get rid of the electronic scoreboard at Fenway and just use that great manually operated one in the Wall. (I've always thought that having an electronic scoreboard at Fenway Park was like having a Rolls Royce and hanging fuzzy dice from the rearview mirror—very tacky.) I'll institute salary caps and revenue sharing. I'll put organic food in the stands, and I'll make it mandatory to serve only cold-pasteurized beer from small, local breweries. No big breweries. Then

> "I remember one time going out to the mound to talk with Bob Gibson. He told me to get back behind the batter; that the only thing I knew about pitching was that it was hard to hit."
>
> —Tim McCarver, former St. Louis Cardinals catcher

I'll bring back warm, roasted peanuts. Just the smell of grass mingled with those roasted peanuts will be enough to draw fans back to the ballparks. Baseball should be an organic game, the way it used to be. It should be about spheroids, not steroids.

In Philadelphia they decided to mix grass with artificial turf. To me, that's the baseball equivalent of hair plugs for men—it doesn't fool anyone and it still makes grown men look silly. At every level except the major leagues, baseball is still the purest and greatest of games. The verities of the game remain timeless and immortal. It's only at that professional pinnacle that all the bastardizations begin. When I see those outrages, I see my own mortality reflected. What we need is a series of mea culpa and more positive thinking.

In the original ballparks, the fields went on forever. Basically you were playing within one Cartesian coordinate of reality. It's a very esoteric thing. You take a circle and cut it into quarters; the plus axis runs up and down, and the minus axis runs left and right. There would be four fields: the plus-plus quadrant, the minus-minus quadrant, and two plus-minus quadrants. You surround yourself with people depending on which quadrant you are in; I always felt that it was the plus-minus axis of reality that held Zimmer back. If he did a positive thing, his negative personality always brought it down. (After a 4–4 road trip, Zimmer once told a reporter: "It could just as easily have gone the other way!") He had to do negative things in negative situations to get positive results. That's the essence of what Descartes was saying: that it is never good to put Descartes in front of de horse. When Descartes died, someone passed by his open coffin and said, "He stinks, therefore he was." They also say that about washed-up major league pitchers who end up playing in outposts like Saskatchewan or Mississippi.

> "A hot dog at the ballpark is better than a steak at the Ritz."
> —Humphrey Bogart

> "Since baseball time is measured only in outs, all you have to do is succeed utterly; keep hitting, keep the rally alive, and you have defeated time. You remain forever young."
> —Roger Angell

Ballplayers, and especially pitchers, are like canaries in the coal mine. Miners used to take canaries down the mine shaft in case there was a whiff of poisonous gas. If there was, the canary would die and the miners would know to get out fast. Similarly, everybody watches ballplayers and benefits from the mistakes we make. We are the barometer for society. Everything affects us and our on-field performance. If there is a whiff of gas, we go down real quick.

You've probably heard of a guy named Mel Famey, a famous Milwaukee Brewers pitcher who walked everyone. He went to a bar one night after a tough loss and got drunk. The Red Sox came into the bar and asked him what beer he was drinking. He took another drink and said, "It's Schlitz." Yastrzemski said, "So that's the beer that made Mel Famey walk us!"

A Chinese professor from Rhode Island used to write me, thinking that because of my last name I was Chinese. He was complaining that NBC announcer Tony Kubek always used to call any dinky little hit to centerfield a "chink hit." He was writing me to make me do something with NBC to make them stop calling it a chink hit. I wrote back and said, "I've got a Chinaman's chance in hell of ever changing that!" But some things in baseball *can* and *should* be changed, and I'm just the guy to do it. And the Boston Red Sox are a great place to start the process rolling. They are one of the original American League teams, and as such they are the canary for all of baseball.

The Trilogy

I have simplified the basic rules of baseball into three categories: the Emotional, the Physical, and the Intellectual. They constitute everything you should know about baseball but might be afraid to ask.

Emotional Rules

1. It's better to be pissed off than pissed on. When Bernie Carbo and Rodney Scott, both easygoing guys, were summarily dismissed by the Red Sox and Expos, respectively, I staged a walkout. I was pissed off; they were pissed off and pissed on.

2. Don't talk about yourself. We'll do that when you leave.

3. Don't false hustle; it detracts from the fact that you can't play. Guys who false hustle become managers; it's a vicious cycle. The truth is Pete Rose, also known as "Charlie Hustle," really did hustle. He loved to play the game. He once said: "I'd walk through hell in a gasoline suit to play baseball."

4. No sycophantism (that means apple polishing, or ass kissing, for those of you without a dictionary).

5. Don't show up your opponent. If you hit a home run, run around the bases with your head down. Ty Cobb was wrong when he said, "The great American game should be an unrelenting war of nerves."

6. Serendipity: believe in the Fates.

7. Remember that the earth is a hanging curveball, and God is doing with it what he wants. He torments Red Sox fans. It's the nature of His personality. Everyone loves to hit a hanger, even God. I hate the word *hanger*. When I was a kid I threw my clothes on the floor, because even then I hated the hanger. I knew it would get me one day. I disdain the hanger.

8. Be confident in your abilities but do *not* alibi. That was the advice my father gave me. Ignore what the great Christy Mathewson once said: "You must have an alibi to show why you lost. If you haven't one, you must fake one. Your self-confidence must be maintained." Pitcher Bo Belinsky, after losing a game 15–0, once said, "How can a guy win a game if you don't give him any runs?"

9. Don't get too high or too low. George Carlin put it best: "Some people think of the glass as half full. Some think of the glass as half empty. I think of the glass as too big." In the early thirties, the Brooklyn Dodgers were perennial National League cellar dwellers, but they still seemed to remain cocky, even arrogant. A New York writer warned

them not to be too cocky: "Overconfidence may cost this team seventh place," he cautioned. At the other extreme is Woody Allen, who once said, "When we played softball, I'd steal second base, feel guilty, and go back."

10. Don't let the other team psych you out like they did Bob Uecker: "When I came up to bat with three men on and two outs in the ninth inning, I looked in the other team's dugout and they were all in street clothes."

Physical Rules

1. If you slide, get up.
2. If you can't play, don't lose your day job.
3. Don't take steroids. If you do, your nuts shrivel up, like Caminiti's. If that happens, make sure you eat a lot of bran flakes to go with your raisins.
4. As young players, we were always lectured about the dangers of women. We were told over and over to stay away from them. Women will make you weak, they said. Well, sex doesn't hurt ballplayers; what hurts is trying to find it at 4:00 in the morning. One of the years that Ferguson Jenkins won 20 games and Vida Blue was winning 20 games, it turns out they were dating the same girl on the road. So they had 20 each, but she had two 20-game winners, making her a 40-game winner, the first 40-game winner since Ed Walsh in 1908.

    Ballplayers are notoriously running into women on the road. I remember Warren Cromartie meeting someone at closing time, and sometimes when the lights are lower, so are your expectations. We were on our knees begging Cro not to go home with that girl. She had a reputation with ballplayers to uphold, and she was really bad lookin'.

    That's where the definition of "coyote ugly" came from. It was coined by guys like Lew Krausse and Marty Pattin. It describes when you wake up in the morning with your arm around a strange girl and you'd rather chew your arm off than move it and wake her up because she's so ugly. Of course, I'm sure women occasionally find themselves in the same predicament. Apparently Pete Rose wouldn't give up on a girl—even if he didn't like her that much anymore—as long as he was still getting base hits. Ah, the superstitions of baseball!

5. When your knuckleball doesn't knuckle, your curveball doesn't curve, and your screwball doesn't screw, it's time to walk away.

6. When your catcher throws the ball back harder than you pitched it, it's time to change your battery—just ask Carlton Fisk. I liked to experiment, but baseball hates experimentation. Fisk wanted to challenge hitters; I wanted to get them out any way I could. I'd throw a change of pace when he was expecting a fastball. He'd get really mad and throw the ball back to me harder than I had thrown it to him. It was embarrassing!

7. Starting is better than relieving. As a starter you get three days to drink and one to recuperate. Relievers pretty much have to be teetotalers all season long.

8. The explosion of home runs in the major leagues is caused by the prevailing southern winds, a result of global warming.

9. Work hard. I went to spring training recently, and I can't believe how easy they have it today. Nothing happens on the field anymore. The players do all their training off the field, I guess with a personal trainer, and then put in a brief appearance on the field. They are a clandestine bunch of guys. They don't want to be approached by the public or the press. They are like Lady Di. They wave to their public, then jump into their limos and disappear. Players must take heed of the wise words of Dave Bristol, former manager of the Milwaukee Brewers, when he said, "There'll be two buses leaving for the ballpark tomorrow.

The 2:00 bus will be for those of you who need a little extra work. The empty bus will leave at 5:00."

10. Ted Williams, the greatest hitter who ever breathed on this earth, had three golden rules of hitting: (1) get a good pitch to hit, (2) be patient, and (3) be quick. For a pitcher, those three golden rules are reversed: (1) don't throw a good pitch to hit, (2) throw strikes on the corners, and (3) throw slow stuff. In short, follow the advice of pitcher Lew Burdette, who said, "I exploit the greed of all hitters."

11. Stay fit and listen to the trainer. Don't let the pressure of the game affect your health the way it did Tommy Lasorda, who admitted, "When we lose, I eat. When we win, I eat. I also eat when we're rained out." Stay healthy. Bob Uecker once claimed, "People don't know it, but I helped the Cardinals win the pennant. I came down with hepatitis. The trainer injected me with it."

12. You are what you eat. Rocky Bridges once explained why he did not eat snails. "I prefer fast food," he said.

13. Yogi said it best: "Baseball is 90 percent mental. The other half is physical." A Texas Rangers manager came to the mound one day to take out pitcher Jim Kern. "I'm not tired," protested Kern. "I know," the manager said, "but the outfielders are exhausted."

Intellectual Rules

1. Always advance runners from second with no outs.
2. Always drive in runners at third with fewer than two outs.
3. Never walk the pitcher. He can't hit a lick. That's why he's called the pitcher.
4. Always play aggressive defense behind a curveball pitcher.
5. Fastballs are fascist; curveballs are democratic. The strikeout is the nonparticipatory part of baseball. It discourages teamwork. The only time you should strike out anyone is if you've got a runner at third with fewer than two outs.

5. A walk may be as good as a hit but at least it's quiet.

6. "If you don't know where you're going, you'll end up somewhere else." —Yogi Berra

7. "Try not! Do, or do not. There is no *try*." —Yoda in *The Empire Strikes Back*

8. If, as Timothy Leary once said, "the universe is an intelligence test," then baseball is little more than a pop quiz.

9. Only complain to the umpire when completely justified; for instance, "Waiter, there's no fly in my soup." —Kermit the Frog

10. Remember, winning is better than the next worse thing.

11. It's bad luck to be behind at the end of the game.

12. Learn about baseball history. Study the craft that gives you such a good living. Most ballplayers don't know the meaning of the word *quit*, but unfortunately they don't know the meaning of many, many other words either.

13. However, it takes more than book learning to be a great ballplayer, as this statement by Gates Brown illustrates: "In high school I took a little English, some science, some hubcaps, and some wheel covers."

CHAPTER 2
Making Red Sox History

I f the "curse of the Bambino," a concept that I planted in *Boston Globe* columnist Dan Shaughnessy's fertile mind some years ago, had not been brought upon the Red Sox, their history could have been quite different. I've always believed that sport and the imagination are inextricably mixed. They nurture one another in a symbiotic sort of way until the line where one ends and the other begins starts to blur. Did Babe Ruth actually point to the center-field bleachers before launching a dramatic home run in that direction, or did we just want him to be that heroic? Did Ty Cobb really sharpen his spikes in order to create mayhem when sliding into second base, or did we just want him to be that villainous?

What young boy has never dreamed of sinking the winning basket in the dying seconds of a championship game, or scoring the winning touchdown for his high school team, or hitting a game-winning homer in the bottom of the ninth? The imagination is cultivated and stimulated by sport; and sport is made much more enjoyable with an assist from the imagination. For fans of a particular team or individual, the fantasizing becomes more focused and more intense. A large part of spectator sport is the vicarious thrill of victory, imagining that you are there, on the field, part of the event. The other joy of sport is visualizing your team celebrating the championship and hoisting the hero of the game on their shoulders.

An active imagination often compensates for the shortcomings of a baseball franchise. The very phrase "Wait 'til next year!" is rooted in imagination. It's what keeps baseball alive in Boston and Chicago. Hot stove leagues are the perfect breeding ground for the imagination to flourish. Dodgers fans fantasize about what a healthy Sandy Koufax might have accomplished in his career. Philadelphia Phillies supporters still imagine a 1964 stretch drive without the infamous swoon. Despite their nauseating string of successes, even Yankees fans dream of a Mickey Mantle without bad knees. And what White Sox fan has not wondered where Shoeless Joe would rank among hitters if he had not been exiled from the game he loved?

The Red Sox have been on a long march since the end of the 1918 season. The years of defeat and defeatist talk, not to mention the advent of MTV and video games, have impaired the imagination of Red Sox fans. When Hideo Nomo pitched his no-hitter in 2001, I saw it on tape a day later and I was *still* on the edge of my seat because, being a Boston fan, I wasn't totally convinced of the outcome until I saw the final out.

It shouldn't be that way. The Bosox are blessed—or cursed—with countless "what if" scenarios. The overriding one is: What if Babe Ruth had not been sold to the New York Yankees? But there is also: What if Ted Williams had not had four-and-a-half years cut from the heart of his career? What if Ted had been traded to the Yankees in exchange for Joe DiMaggio? What if the Green Monster was not a feature of Fenway Park? What if it was located in right field instead of left field? What if the Red Sox had not been the last major league team to sign a black player, but the first? What if Tony Conigliaro hadn't been struck in the head by a Jack Hamilton fastball during the 1967 season? What if Bill Buckner had been lifted for defensive purposes in the tenth inning of Game 6 of the 1986 World Series? What if Roger

Clemens had been able to play out his entire career in Boston, instead of going to New York to get his World Series ring like some 54th Street hooker?

What if Red Sox manager Darrell Johnson had not pinch-hit for Jim Willoughby in the eighth inning of Game 7 of the 1975 World Series? What if Mel Parnell and not Denny Galehouse had pitched the 1948 playoff game against the Cleveland Indians? What if Jim Lonborg had taken up chess instead of skiing? What if Ellis Kinder and Mickey McDermott had been teetotalers? What if Dom DiMaggio had been in center field at the end of Game 7 in 1946? What if Bucky Dent had never been born, or had taken up the piano instead of baseball? What if umpire Larry Barnett had called interference on Ed Armbrister? What if we had turned the double play on Johnny Bench's hard roller to short in the

Before a game at Fenway Park, Yankees manager Joe McCarthy found his ace southpaw Lefty Gomez sitting in a phone booth outside the park. Lefty explained it this way: "Now when I get in there and go out to the mound, the place will seem huge."

Aside from being one of the best relievers in baseball history, Sparky Lyle used to like to drop his pants and sit on birthday cakes. Everyone has to have a hobby, and that was his. He once made the mistake of sitting on Tom Yawkey's cake, and Mr. Yawkey did not see the humor in it. The very next day Sparky was shipped to New York in exchange for Danny Cater. (In spring training Cater was lying on the ground after being brushed back and hit on the bill of his helmet. He said, "I can't see! I can't see." George Scott, who was on deck, looked down and said, "Well open up your eyes.") What if Sparky Lyle hadn't sat on Tom Yawkey's birthday cake? He wouldn't have followed Ruth's ghost to New York.

1975 Series? What if Denny Doyle had played closer to second base? What if Yaz hadn't stretched too soon? What if Doyle's throw hadn't gone into the Red Sox dugout? Then, I wouldn't have thrown that slow hanging curve to Tony Perez and he wouldn't have hit it out.

What if fate hadn't dealt the Red Sox one cruel blow after another? But, as Johnny Carson once said, "If life was fair, Elvis would be alive and all the impersonators would be dead."

I have an active imagination. I once imagined that my manager resembled a gerbil. I also imagined that the Red Sox would show some loyalty to Bernie Carbo and that the Green Monster was just an alcohol-induced mirage. Now I get to put my imagination to practical use. If George Burns can play Hollywood's version of God, who better to play the role in baseball than Chairman Lee? Like an errant fastball accidentally thrown into the Yankees' dugout, each event causes a chain reaction, a ripple effect of amazing proportions—and I hope you'll stick around for the ride.

> There's nothing in the world like the fatalism of the Red Sox fans, which has been bred into them for generations by that little green ballpark and the Wall, and by a team that keeps trying to win by hitting everything out of sight and just out-bombarding everyone else in the league. All this makes Boston fans a little crazy, and I'm sorry for them.

Chapter 3

Throwing the Babe Out with the Bathwater

*"Forget about finding Ruth's piano, his organ
holds the key to reversing the curse."*

—Chairman Lee

More than half a century after his death, Babe Ruth's name continues to symbolize baseball around the world. In New York, it is a name that represents the genesis of the most incredible dynasty since the Mings of China put together that impressive winning streak. In Japan, China, Cuba, the Dominican Republic, Latin America, and everywhere else that baseball is played, "Ruth" is a synonym for baseball excellence. During World War II, Japanese soldiers taunted American GIs with cries of "To Hell with Babe Ruth!" (If the two countries ever go to war again, American GIs will no doubt be shouting, "Sayonara Ichiro!")

In America, Babe Ruth is a part of our history and our folklore. The man with the big belly and skinny legs is the Santa Claus of our national sport. He is as real as his statistics and as legendary as Paul Bunyan or John Henry (the steel driving man, not the Red Sox owner or Ted Williams' offspring). His feats are known on every playground and sandlot from my hometown of

> "If I ever became
> commissioner, I'd
> immediately fire all
> the owners."
>
> —Chairman Lee

Burbank, California, to Bunyan's hometown of Bangor, Maine. His name is revered across the length and breadth of the land.

But in one supposedly enlightened northeastern U.S. city, the very mention of his name evokes a bittersweet response. In Boston he is more Grinch than Santa, more Benedict Arnold than Paul Revere. The reason? In December of 1919, the Red Sox sold Babe Ruth to the New York Yankees for $100,000 and a $300,000 mortgage on Fenway Park. (And I thought it was a bad deal when I was traded for Stan Papi.) Not that I am comparing myself to Babe Ruth; although we were both pretty good southpaw pitchers, he was a somewhat better hitter than I was. It was baseball's version of selling Manhattan to the Native Americans in exchange for some costume jewelry. New York got the gold mine and the Red Sox got the shaft. The event could not have been more devastating for Boston if Harvard University had decided to relocate to the Bronx, the U.S.S. *Constitution* weighed anchor and made the East River her new home port, or the Boston Pops signed on as David Letterman's house band.

If history were different, I don't think the Babe would have had the bad rap he got as a hell-raiser. He was such a lovable guy. He was happy with his new wife until he went to New York. She was a waitress from Nova Scotia, and they bought a little place out in Sudbury, Massachusetts. He was a gentleman farmer like me. I've often said that Vermont saved my life, because if I'd continued to live in Montreal with all the temptations it offers, I'd be dead. Same thing with Ruth being banished from Boston to New York. New York chewed him up and spit him out, and when he tried to come back to be a manager, they wouldn't hire him. They just wanted him to be part of some cheap sideshow, hitting baseballs into the ocean. Baseball owners like sideshows. That's why

Pedro Martinez doubted the existence of the curse of the Bambino. He even went so far as to say, "Dig Babe up and let me pitch to him, and I'll drill him in the butt." The next day Pedro's arm fell off and his season was essentially over. That's what happens when you defy the curse and disrespect the Babe. The curse was at work once again. Boston is a hotbed of witchcraft, and witches and warlocks are on every corner. They can be malevolent or benevolent. It all depends on how they are treated. To alleviate that curse, you have to treat them with respect.

Charles Finley had his mule. That's why they dressed me up in a space suit for the cover of *Sports Illustrated*. If he had remained in Boston, Ruth would have become a New England icon and he would have been a part of the Boston baseball scene forever.

In 1990, I got a phone call from WZLX, a new rock 'n' roll radio station in Boston. Charles Laquidara, who had the morning show, brought me down to break the curse of the Bambino. They wanted me to drive to Boston and back, from Vermont, for the grand sum of $500. I said, "OK, I'll come, but I can't stay to watch the ballgame." The Red Sox were playing the Toronto Blue Jays.

Before the game they had an effigy of Babe Ruth in the Twins souvenir shop across from the ballpark, on what was Jersey Street when Ruth played there. Paul Poirier, a warlock, showed up in his full regalia along with Laurie Cabot, New England's best-known witch. They had a broken bat with them, and they began to chant the sort of mumbo-jumbo incantations that you always hear in séances. They said: "We heal the spirit of Babe Ruth. This bat represents his broken spirit and we heal

(continued on next page)

it." And then they presented the bat to me, as a representative of the Red Sox and of all those years of frustration.

I had parked in the team parking lot because I knew the guy who ran it and they let me park there. I put the broken bat in the trunk of my car to take home with me. The organizers talked me into watching a couple of innings of the game, so I ran back into the ballpark to watch the first inning. It was Roger Clemens for the Red Sox against Todd Stottlemyre for the Blue Jays, and Tom Brunansky was at bat. Brunansky had only been with the Red Sox a short time, having just come over from St. Louis. He got jammed with the bases loaded and hit the ball to Stottlemyre, who threw home for the force, and the Blue Jays catcher threw to first to double off the runner. The Red Sox failed to score in the bottom of the first and it was 0–0. Clemens was pitching and he was throwing BBs! I said the heck with it and left. I had the game on in the car, and just as I was going over the Mystic River, Brunansky got up again and hit a home run. I got up around Laconia, and he hit a second home run in his third at-bat. Then, in his fourth at-bat, as I was going over the Franconia Notch, descending into the Northeast Kingdom, I suddenly couldn't hear for the static so I switched over to WTIC out of Hartford, which reaches up the Connecticut River. Finally I got the Red Sox station there, and the Blue Jays had brought in a young rookie reliever. The reliever threw a low fastball on a 3–1 count, and Brunansky hit his third home run of the game! When I got home and pulled into the driveway, I opened the trunk and looked at the bat that they gave me. It was a Tom Brunansky bat! Honest to God! He hadn't even been with them long enough to crack a bat, so how did they get hold of one? Brunansky is from Covina, California. Get it? Was he from Covina—or from a *coven?*

(continued on next page)

The thing is that these fans had petitioned the two witches to help the Red Sox beat Toronto and win the American League East title. We want to beat Toronto! Well, they did that! They beat Toronto. They won the AL East, and then they lost four straight in the American League Championship Series to Oakland. In other words, if they had asked the witches to win the AL pennant or the World Series . . . But that's the narrow-mindedness and shortsightedness of the New England fans. They are limited by their own imaginations. When you have fate and destiny right there and you have a chance to ask for what you want, you don't know what you want. It's part of the conservative ethic of the New England fans. The fatalism of Red Sox fans has been bred into them since the time of the Salem witch trials. It is why we maintain a tiny green ballpark and a wall just beyond third base that makes every right-handed hitter pull the ball whether he should or not. That's the curse of the Bambino. I was there. I saw it play out time after time.

In 1975 I saw Laurie Cabot dance on the dugout in Cleveland in a rain delay, and we ended up winning something like 18 in a row, going coast to coast. But we didn't win the World Series that year either. When it gets down to the nitty-gritty, to alleviate that curse in the sixth or seventh game of the World Series, you're talking a lot of power. And the witches aren't always on our side. In the '86 World Series, the New York Mets fans who were spinning their hands behind home plate in Shea Stadium in New York were witches! That's exactly what that symbol is! They were demons from New York who were trying to suck the power out of Calvin Schiraldi and Bob Stanley. That's why it's so true when they say that New York sucks! That's my theory; Ruth was pulling for the Mets. It all fits in with the curse.

It is no exaggeration to suggest that Ruth's departure altered Boston history to a very significant extent. When he departed, a little bit of the city's self-esteem went with him. And despite the fact that Boston is America's acknowledged center of academic enlightenment, it has never returned. It was as if Babe was a pied piper, luring other Boston institutions out of town with him. Coincidence or not, banks began to make the move to New York, prestigious publishing houses decided to relocate there, and so did prominent businesses such as Macy's. Soon Boston was a poor cousin of the metropolis to the south.

The history of Babe Ruth's brief time with the Red Sox is almost stranger than fiction. He first played under owner Joe Lannin, but after winning the 1916 World Series, Lannin wanted to sell the club. One of the interested buyers was Joseph Kennedy, patriarch of what was to become America's foremost political family, but his bid fell short. Instead, Harry Frazee, a New York theater man, purchased the Boston Red Sox Baseball Club in December of 1916—in the midst of the first World War—a bold move not inconsistent with Frazee's flair for the dramatic.

Red Sox fans were initially pleased with the new ownership. They quickly saw that Frazee was a man of action. This impression was helped along by Frazee's willingness to open his wallet to bring in a new cast of players. Frazee was an outsider from the effete world of theater, and he treated baseball as he would a Broadway production.

In a blockbuster deal with the financially ailing Philadelphia A's, he added pitcher Joe Bush, catcher Walter Schang, and outfielder Amos Strunk. At the time, it was the biggest single deal in baseball history. Shortly after, Frazee also brought New England native Stuffy McInnis over from the A's. Red Sox fans heaved a collective sigh of relief. It looked as though Frazee was raising the curtain on a whole new era of Red Sox success.

The Red Sox had won the World Series in 1915 and 1916 but finished second in the AL pennant race in 1917 under the new ownership. Frazee promptly hired Ed Barrow as his manager, and the rejuvenated Red Sox rebounded to win the Series again in 1918, their fifth championship since the competition began in 1903 and the third with Babe Ruth leading the charge. Frazee relished the

> "The game has a cleanness. If you do a good job, the numbers say so. You don't have to ask anyone or play politics. You don't have to wait for the reviews."
>
> —Sandy Koufax

victory. The World Series was baseball's "Great White Way" and all his actors had performed well on opening night. Babe Ruth was the headliner, but Frazee fancied himself the director, producer, and choreographer all rolled into one.

■ ■ ■

The Red Sox had acquired Ruth, along with pitcher Ernie Shore and catcher Ben Egan, from the minor league Baltimore Orioles for less than $10,000, an amazing bargain. The 19-year-old Ruth was then a muscular 6'2", 200-pound pitching prospect who also showed some promise as a hitter. He featured tremendous arm speed, and he overpowered hitters. He was not a Bill Lee kind of finesse pitcher, more of a Clemens power pitcher. Much to the surprise of everyone, he also batted .315 and hit four homers in just 92 at-bats in his freshman campaign. The league leader in home runs that season had seven. In today's game it would be like having Pedro Martinez and Manny Ramirez all rolled into one.

In his first three major league seasons, Ruth the ace pitcher had rung up records of 18–8, 23–12, and 23–13. In 1916, his ERA was a microscopic 1.75. In 1918 he divided his time between pitching and playing the outfield. Ruth the hitter responded with a league-leading 11 homers. The Red Sox won the pennant and the World Series and seemed on the verge of becoming a dynasty. On

November 11 the "war to end all wars" officially ended, and the future looked bright. Unfortunately, the Red Sox victory that year was to be the "win to end all wins." But no one in Boston could have imagined such a thing. Optimism reigned. There was an offer from New York for Babe Ruth for $100,000, but Frazee, still flush with both money and success, nixed it.

One warm summer night—it could have been late July, maybe early August (the dog days of summer had come early in Massachusetts)—the maples were in full canopy and there was scarcely a breath of wind to disturb the leaves. The thunderstorms that would cut the closeness were still lurking out past the Berkshires. Babe Ruth sat on his porch. The lightning bugs, the glow of a half-smoked cigar, and the fire in his eyes provided the only light in the muggy darkness. The year was 1919, and the Ruths had gone out to their small cottage on the pond near the Wayland-Sudbury line. I can envision Babe's first wife, Helen, trying to console him after a tough loss that very afternoon. She is inside attempting to play a nocturne by Chopin on their new piano, a gift from the Babe made possible by the World Series share that he knew was coming.

The sound is wafting through the open window. Despite her best efforts to soothe her Babe with a lullaby, she apparently hit a discordant note. Exactly what set him off is open to conjecture. Was it because he just suffered a 2–1 loss on an error by the shortstop? Or maybe because with two outs and the runner at third, he was late covering first, allowing the winning run to score. ("Fundamentals, Tiger!" USC coach Rod Dedeaux used to say, "Fundamentals!")

How did he go from being a happy-go-lucky guy to that dark side? Whatever it was, in a fit of temper, Babe threw his wife's piano into the adjacent lake. It was a Herculean feat. After

(continued on next page)

going nine innings in 100-degree heat, downing 12 Narragansetts, and eating one-quarter of a suckling pig, he was still able to skip that piano across the pond past the lily pads before it went under in two fathoms of water. Only a fellow southpaw can relate to that degree of anger and frustration. Only a fellow southpaw can surmise what caused him to throw that piano into the lake. Usually my fits of anger are spontaneous and fleeting. I shoot my mouth off and then forget it. This one had to be premeditated and prolonged and must have involved some buddies—maybe the infielder who made the error—because punching a water cooler is one thing, throwing a piano into a lake is on a far grander scale (excuse the double piano pun).

So now that we've located the piano, will the curse of the Bambino be lifted? We've tried before. I think not. Witch Laurie Cabot, warlock Paul Poirier, and I tried in the nineties with Brunansky's bat. We would have succeeded if not for the short-sightedness of WZLX and the Boston fans. My friend Mike Adams, a Boston news commentator, said it best: "It's good that they don't go looking for his organ." Well, maybe they should. Finding where his organ has been may be the key to reversing the curse. Across New England, there must be scores of Babe Ruth's great-great-grand-bambinos just waiting to be recruited to the Red Sox.

And then it happened. Disillusioned with the politics of baseball, Frazee began to sell off many of his star players. Thus weakened, the Red Sox abruptly fell to a sixth-place finish in 1919. Despite Boston's free fall in the AL standings, fans continued to come out to see the Babe. In Frazee's lingo, he was "boffo at the box office." And with good reason. In 1919 he performed a miracle of sorts by raising the dead: he lifted 29 lifeless baseballs out of American League ballparks. His three-year total from 1917 to 1919 was a then eye-popping 42 home runs.

Despite this unheard-of feat, Frazee made the decision to sell the Babe and rid himself of his disruptive influence on the team. There was some justification for his impatience with the Babe's shenanigans. Ruth had been involved in a number of on-field and off-field incidents that had embarrassed Frazee and the organization. But this scarcely excused the worst deal in baseball history. The reaction to the transaction in Boston was immediate and predictable. Frazee was instantly vilified and, indeed, is still despised in New England to this very day.

Ruth's arrival in New York coincided with the arrival in baseball of the lively ball. Ruth promptly hit 54 homers, batted .376, and drove in 137 runs. He followed that, in 1921, with 59 homers, 171 RBIs, and a .378 average. He reached his apex of achievement in 1927 by powering 60 homers. His career totals are awesome in the truest sense of that overworked word. The baseball record books tell us that Ruth led the American League in home runs 12 times, averaging more than 40 a year during that sustained barrage. From 1926 to the beginning of his hitting "decline" in 1932 (he still hit 41 homers that year), he averaged more than 50 home runs per year! His career totals were 714 home runs, 2,213 RBIs, a .690 slugging average, and a .342 batting average over 22 major league seasons.

Ruth went on to lead the Yankees to seven pennants and four World Series championships. He probably saved baseball from ruination after the Black Sox scandal tarnished the integrity of the game. He is personally responsible for the construction of Yankee Stadium, and he was the impetus behind, and the cornerstone of, the Yankees dynasty that followed—a dynasty that has continued with but a few interruptions to this very day. He revolutionized the game with his ability to hit home runs. He brought the fans out in record numbers and enabled the Yankees to build on their success, signing such names as Gehrig, DiMaggio, and eventually Mantle.

■　■　■

When Joseph Patrick Kennedy was a boy, his father, Patrick Joseph Kennedy, a passionate baseball fan, played catch with him for hours on end. He took his son to virtually all the home games of the Boston Red Sox. This love of baseball never left young Joe, and throughout his life he followed with keen interest the fortunes of the Sox.

In 1912, Joe Kennedy graduated from Harvard and looked to the future. In 1914, the same year that Ruth arrived in Boston from Baltimore, Kennedy was elected president of Columbia Trust, a company owned by his father. He also married Rose Fitzgerald, the daughter of Boston mayor John Fitzgerald.

In 1917, with war raging in Europe and Joe classified as fit and able to fight for his country, his father-in-law secured a position for him at Bethlehem Shipbuilding Corporation. The crucial nature of the work done at the Quincy Plant kept him from the battlefield. When Joe became assistant general manager of Bethlehem Steel's Fore River Shipyard outside of Boston, his baseball interest took an immediate and practical turn. The Bethlehem Steel Baseball League was a highly competitive circuit, perhaps second only to the American and National Leagues! Kennedy's employer pressured the young executive to field a worthy team. Kennedy's own competitive streak kicked in, and the battle for players raged. During World War I, Bethlehem Steel was extremely aggressive in raiding the major league teams for the best available players to augment the rosters of its network of plants.

> "Freedom of the press is limited to those who own one."
>
> —A. J. Liebling

The father of young Joe Jr. and John Fitzgerald had gotten a taste of baseball wheeling and dealing, and it appealed to his competitive nature. Little wonder that he had looked at the Red

My first impulse is to say that if Kennedy had taken over, it could have been even more tragic for the Red Sox. Oh God, just think which player would have been in the back of Ted's car and would have died in Chappaquiddick. Clemens might never have made it off the island! Just think if all the ballplayers hung around the Kennedys. They would be even worse than they are now! Oh, the scandals! They would have been hanging around with Marilyn Monroe—and Ted Williams, not Joe DiMaggio, would have married Marilyn. And Henry Miller, not Arthur Miller, would have married her next. She would have dyed her hair blue and still been alive today. This song by Dan Bern (the new Bob Dylan), called "Marilyn," says it all.

Marilyn
by Dan Bern

Marilyn Monroe didn't marry Henry Miller
Marilyn Monroe didn't marry Henry Miller
Marilyn Monroe didn't marry Henry Miller
Marilyn Monroe didn't marry Henry Miller

But if she did
He'd a taken her to Paris
And if she did
She'd have smoked a lot of opium
And if she did
She'd have dyed her hair blue
And if she did
She might be alive

Oh-ohh Henry Miller
Oh-ohh Marilyn Monroe
Oh-ohh Henry Miller
Oh-ohh Marilyn Monroe

(continued on next page)

Marilyn Monroe didn't marry Henry Miller
She lived outside the Tropic of Capricorn
Marilyn Monroe didn't marry Henry Miller
I don't even know if she knew Henry Miller

But if she did
He'd a taken her to Paris
And if she did
They'd have fucked every day
And if she did
She'd have felt like a woman
Not a photograph
In a magazine

Oh-ohh Henry Miller
Oh-ohh Marilyn Monroe

This is not a knock against Arthur Miller
Death of a Salesman is my favorite play
But Marilyn Monroe
Should have married Henry Miller
And if she did
She might be alive

Cause if she did
He'd have taken her to Paris
Tied her to the bed
And eaten dinner off of her
And okay maybe
she'd have died the same, anyway
But if she did
she'd have had more fun

Oh-ohh Henry Miller
Oh-ohh Marilyn Monroe
Oh-ohh Henry Miller
Oh-ohh Marilyn Monroe

Sox and in 1916 decided to mount a bid to purchase the team. While Frazee's ownership bid had succeeded instead, Kennedy was able to use the Fore River situation to satisfy at least some of his baseball ambitions.

Perhaps this brief—and risk-free—foray into baseball was enough to satisfy Kennedy, perhaps not. In any case, his goals evolved and changed, and he moved to New York, where his pursuits often took him to fields less pure, and with many more facets, than the diamond variety.

Babe Ruth and Joe Kennedy were only seven years apart in age (Kennedy was born in 1888, Ruth in 1895) and despite very different backgrounds, they were both much, much larger than life. Both were American success stories, Horatio Alger figures who helped to forge the American character. As a would-be movie entrepreneur in late autumn of 1919, Kennedy attempted to sign Babe Ruth to star in a film that his studio was making. Ironically, at almost the same time, that other Boston theatrical entrepreneur, the man named Frazee, was mere months from dumping his Falstaffian slugger from the Red Sox cast and moving him out of Boston. The Ruth-Kennedy collaboration never happened. Nevertheless, in a city the size of Boston, this interaction between two budding behemoths like Kennedy and Ruth is, at the very least, fascinating.

When the Eighteenth Amendment, prohibiting the manufacture, transport, and import of "intoxicating liquors," was ratified on January 29, 1919, Kennedy's life took another turn. He purchased booze from offshore suppliers and used illegal organizations to market it. Kennedy quickly became a millionaire and used his liquor money to invest in the stock market, as well as in his film ventures. By the time Prohibition was repealed in the early thirties, Kennedy had all the right contacts for the importation and distribution of again-legal liquor products.

Kennedy's burgeoning business career continued to parallel Ruth's blossoming baseball rise. They were two legendary giants developing side by side in the same fertile New England environment. Their backgrounds and upbringing could not have been more different, and yet each was equal parts man and myth. Both were darlings of the media. Neither was a saint. Both attacked life with gusto, and neither was afraid to challenge the status quo. Their paths crossed briefly, but nothing substantial came of it. What if they had pooled their resources as owner and star of the Red Sox? What if Ruth had been a lifelong Red Sox player? What if the curse of the Bambino had never damned the fans of Boston?

If Kennedy had bought the Red Sox, Prohibition might have gone on forever. Joe made his money smuggling booze, and he'd want that to continue. The Boston Braves would have become the Milwaukee Milquetoasts, and instead of Busch Stadium, the Cardinals would be playing in Botanical Garden and serve herbal tea instead of Bud.

Joe Kennedy became one of the most successful and influential businessmen in America, and his family was soon to be elevated to the status of American royalty. Almost simultaneously Ruth was to become the King of Clout and the Sultan of Swat.

Both Kennedy and Ruth were builders of dynasties: Kennedy's were financial and political; Ruth's were confined to baseball. Kennedy sold illegal beer and Babe consumed it in astonishing quantities. One fact is impossible to dispute: the departure of Babe Ruth spelled the abrupt end of one dynasty and the spectacular beginning of another. At the time Babe left for the Big Apple, the Red Sox had won six American League pennants and five World Series. In the ensuing 85 years, they have won four AL flags and no world championships. New York is associated with the Babe and winning. Boston is associated with the Babe and losing. "Everything would have been different if he had remained in Boston," former Speaker of the House Tip O'Neill

> I've often thought of writing and staging a play called *The Year I Owned the Red Sox*. Act One would have me and the Red Sox groundskeeper digging up Babe Ruth's body, like a scene from Shakespeare's *Hamlet*. It would be a cloak-and-dagger kind of thing. I would hold up his skull and paraphrase the Bard: "Alas, poor Babe, I know his homer ratio." I'd secretly carry the body back to Boston and bury it under the mound at Fenway Park. Surely that would appease the gods. It would also make the mound higher, always a good thing for pitchers, dead or alive.

once opined. The real frustration in Boston is that the New York Yankees teams that began the dynasty were really the Boston Red Sox in pinstripes. There but for the (dis)grace of Frazee went us.

If Kennedy and Ruth had worked together, they might have created the greatest baseball dynasty in the history of the diamond. Unfortunately, their career paths did not converge. . . .

But what if . . .

As odd couples go, Joe Kennedy and Harry Frazee made Felix and Oscar look like identical twins. Kennedy, an opportunistic Irishman with a pioneering spirit, had heard rumors that the Red Sox owner was about to dismantle the "Olde Towne Team" by selling off its star performers. Joe had two young boys, Joe Jr. and Jack, and he believed totally in the American dream. He knew that this dream would be handed to no man; it must be won through blood, sweat, tears—and if necessary—by bending the rules to the breaking point. The shrewd young businessman thought the time was right to make a move to buy the Boston Red Sox.

Rumors of Ruth's pending sale to the Yankees made Frazee the most unpopular man in Boston. Even Will Rogers said he couldn't abide the man. In 1916, Frazee had outbid Kennedy's group for ownership of the Red Sox, and the franchise had initially fared pretty well during the theatrical owner's stewardship.

But Frazee had soured on baseball and Boston, and especially on troublemakers like Babe Ruth. He knew something about bad actors, and Ruth was definitely a bad actor. Frazee's heart was a few hundred miles away in New York. He was hoping to get a fair price for his team but would have been quite happy to sell it at cost. He dreamed of being back among his acting friends and away from Beantown, a city that was much too parochial, too stuffy, and too academic for his tastes.

Babe Ruth's Red Sox Pitching/Hitting Record

- **1914:** W-2, L-1/3.91 ERA/0 HR/2 RBI/.200 AVG
  Red Sox Finish: second
  Yankees Finish: sixth
- **1915:** W-18, L-8/2.44 ERA/4 HR/21 RBI/.315 AVG
  Red Sox Finish: first (won World Series)
  Yankees Finish: fifth
- **1916:** W-23, L-12/1.75 ERA*/3 HR/15 RBI/.272 AVG
  Red Sox Finish: first (won World Series)
  Yankees Finish: fourth
- **1917:** W-24, L-13/2.01 ERA/2 HR/12 RBI/.325 AVG
  Red Sox Finish: second
  Yankees Finish: sixth
- **1918:** W-13, L-7/2.22 ERA/11 HR*/66 RBI/.300 AVG
  Red Sox Finish: first (won World Series)
  Yankees Finish: fourth
- **1919:** W-9, L-5/2.97 ERA/29 HR*/114 RBI*/.322 AVG
  Red Sox Finish: sixth
  Yankees Finish: third (Frazee was in the midst of
    unloading star players)

*denotes led league

Note: Ruth helped lead the Red Sox to two American League pennants and two World Series championships in his six years in Boston.

Babe Ruth's Yankee Hitting Record

- **1920:** 54 HR*/137 RBI*/.376 AVG
  Yankees Finish: third
  Red Sox Finish: fifth
- **1921:** 59 HR*/171 RBI*/.378 AVG
  Yankees Finish: first
  Red Sox Finish: fifth
- **1922:** 35 HR/99 RBI/.315 AVG
  Yankees Finish: first
  Red Sox Finish: eighth (last)
- **1923:** 41 HR*/131 RBI*/.393 AVG
  Yankees Finish: first (won World Series)
  Red Sox Finish: eighth (last)
- **1924:** 46 HR*/121 RBI/.378 AVG*
  Yankees Finish: second
  Red Sox Finish: seventh
- **1925:** 25 HR/66 RBI/.290 AVG
  Yankees Finish: seventh
  Red Sox Finish: eighth (last)
- **1926:** 47 HR*/146 RBI*/.372 AVG
  Yankees Finish: first
  Red Sox Finish: eighth (last)
- **1927:** 60 HR*/164 RBI*/.356 AVG
  Yankees Finish: first (won World Series)
  Red Sox Finish: eighth (last)
- **1928:** 54 HR*/142 RBI*/.323 AVG
  Yankees Finish: first (won World Series)
  Red Sox Finish: eighth (last)
- **1929:** 46 HR*/154 RBI/.345 AVG
  Yankees Finish: second
  Red Sox Finish: eighth (last)

(continued on next page)

- **1930:** 49 HR*/153 RBI/.359 AVG

    Yankees Finish: third

    Red Sox Finish: eighth (last)
- **1931:** 46 HR*/163 RBI/.373 AVG

    Yankees Finish: second

    Red Sox Finish: sixth
- **1932:** 41 HR/137 RBI/.341 AVG

    Yankees Finish: first (won World Series)

    Red Sox Finish: eighth (last)
- **1933:** 34 HR/103 RBI/.301 AVG

    Yankees Finish: second

    Red Sox Finish: seventh
- **1934:** 22 HR/84 RBI/.288 AVG

    Yankees Finish: second

    Red Sox Finish: fourth

*denotes led league

Notes:
- Ruth's pitching record with New York was limited to five appearances over four seasons; he won all five games.
- Ruth led the Yankees to seven American League pennants and four World Series championships in his 15 seasons in New York.
- Ruth finished his career in 1935 as a member of the National League's Boston Braves, where he managed six home runs, 12 RBIs, and a .181 average in 28 games.

Frazee had also entered into negotiations with Yankees owner Jacob Ruppert, and in fact Ruppert seemed likely to be the winning bidder, until the looming threat of Prohibition caused the New York brewer to back off. Meanwhile, what was a threat to Ruppert was a potential godsend to Kennedy. Prohibition would be like a license to print money for this ambitious son-in-law of Boston mayor John Fitzgerald. The Red Sox would give him a respectable front for his smuggling and bootlegging activities, while raising his social profile in Boston. When Prohibition ended, as it inevitably must, he would be well positioned to go legit and use his expertise to corner the liquor market, with Fenway Park as the cornerstone of his business, his credibility, and his veneer of respectability.

The two men did not mince words. Kennedy was determined to succeed where he had previously failed. He made an offer that reflected the market value of the Red Sox. Frazee admired his bravado, and after only a brief discussion, the offer was accepted. They parted ways with a handshake, agreeing to let their financial people iron out the details. Within seven days, the deal had been signed, sealed, and delivered. AL president Ban Johnson was openly supportive of the deal. Never a friend of Frazee's, he was pleased to have the new Red Sox owner in place, and the original Kennedy-Johnson ticket was born.

Kennedy had come by his wealth in a variety of ways, some within the legal strike zone and some well low and outside, but all colorful, all larger than life. He was a man who knew what he wanted and allowed nothing to get in his way. Less than two weeks after Kennedy bought the Red Sox on January 29, 1919, the Eighteenth Amendment, prohibiting the making, marketing, transporting, and importing of beverage alcohol, was ratified. Once again Joe Kennedy had seen an opportunity and grasped it. He celebrated with a cup of hot chocolate.

Baseball and booze had a long history; they had been cohorts from the very beginnings of the game. The Red Sox would scarcely be unique in being sponsored by brewers and distillers, but they were surely the only ones to hold this distinction during Prohibition! Kennedy had associations with criminal syndicates in such centers as New York, Boston, and Chicago. He brought in booze from Europe and delivered it to these underground contacts at a handsome profit. This smuggling ring was highly organized and sophisticated, and it involved well-known mobsters. At this point the Red Sox would be only indirect beneficiaries of the liquor trade, but once Prohibition ended, Kennedy would have the perfect infrastructure in place to make the family business legitimate. It was a symbiotic relationship: the money from the sale of Kennedy's illegal booze would enable him to keep players such as Ruth in Boston and, in the case of Ruth, keep him happy while there. Around the speakeasies of Boston, the joke would soon be that Kennedy bootlegged just enough liquor to keep his star player happy. Other wags suggested that Ruth drank up all of Kennedy's profits. The bootlegger and the Bambino were another odd couple.

■ ■ ■

Kennedy's first priority as the new owner was clear. He had to secure his franchise player to a long-term contract. He called George Herman "Babe" Ruth into his office, and the two men exchanged pleasantries before getting down to business.

Kennedy knew that Frazee and Ruth had been at odds over the past few years and was aware that Frazee had openly called his star player a "handicap and not an asset." Kennedy didn't see it that way at all. To him, Ruth was the most attractive asset of the Red Sox purchase, more important even than Fenway Park itself. He knew talent when he saw it. He also could spot a person who had star quality; it's a talent that Frazee should have possessed, but for him such insights were limited to actors and actresses. He could not—or chose not to—see the Babe in that light. Kennedy, on the other hand, knew that Ruth was on the verge of the kind of stardom that America had seldom seen in its sporting heroes. He had more raw talent than Cobb and, with his fun-loving personality, was much more marketable to the public than temperamental Ty. After all, the Roaring Twenties were about to be launched, and the gregarious Ruth was far more reflective of the postwar spirit than the nasty and sinister Cobb.

Ruth was no matinee idol in the conventional sense, but he was charismatic and larger than life, and all he needed was the right person to handle him. Babe was already as popular as any movie star Hollywood had to offer. He doffed his hat to the crowd after every home run, and he signed autographs by the hundreds for kids in all American League ballparks. His love of people, and especially children, was genuine. The impact of Babe's drinking and womanizing could be minimized or even turned to advantage, be made to seem colorful, by a man with Kennedy's promotional abilities and media connections. In Boston, having a few drinks had never been considered a bad thing. It just made the Babe one of them.

Kennedy knew how to promote talent to get the very most out of it. He could make Ruth an icon in Boston and across America. He knew how to handle the press. He could sell this baseball vagrant as baseball's rags-to-riches orphan. He already had dreams that one of his sons would someday be president of the United States. Making Babe Ruth into an icon was child's play for a man with such dreams and ambitions.

■ ■ ■

Ruth had won nine games and lost five with a 2.97 ERA for the Red Sox in 1919. In his six years in Boston he boasted a superb mound record of 89–46. But it wasn't pitching that was on Kennedy's mind. Ruth had set the baseball world on its collective ear during the 1919 season, with a record 29 home runs, 114 RBIs, and a .322 batting average. Baseball fans were intrigued. Where they once came to the ballpark to see pitching and station-to-station offense, they were now coming to see Babe hit the long ball. Kennedy was always the first to spot an opportunity, and his business instincts were practically infallible.

"George, I see big things for you in Boston. You can become a big name here, a very big name indeed. Boston can become your town. I can help you. I have Hollywood connections and I have newspaper connections. We can make you into a national hero. Bigger than Cobb or any of them."

"Thanks, Mr. Kennedy. I certainly like Boston and I'd love to stay here, but the price has to be right and I have to get a few other things straight."

"Like what, Babe?" said Kennedy.

"Number one, I want to be an everyday ballplayer. I can hit that old tomato pretty good, and to be honest it's my ticket as far as I'm concerned. I can pitch too, but I want to play every day. I can do both. I want to do both. And I want to be paid accordingly. After all, you'll be getting two players for the price of one!"

"You read my mind, George," said a grinning Kennedy. "You read my mind."

"You mean you don't object?" said the Babe.

"Object?" countered Kennedy. "Why, I wouldn't have it any other way. Let's have a drink to seal the deal." Kennedy reached into the bottom drawer of his oak desk. The Babe's eyes widened. "What do you have there?" he asked. In response, Kennedy plunked a 40-ounce bottle of seven-year-old Scotch on the desk and splashed generous portions into two crystal tumblers. "In keeping with the double duty you'll be pulling, I think you deserve a double!" he grinned. "Here's to the Ruth era in Boston!"

"I'll drink to that," said Ruth, downing the amber liquid in a single gulp and belching loudly.

Kennedy's first move as owner was to double Ruth's salary to a record $20,000, surpassing the previous high of $17,000 earned by Eddie Collins. Babe positively glowed when he heard the news. He had always loved Boston and had never wanted to leave the city that had embraced him so warmly. Frazee had flatly rejected previous Ruth requests for a large raise, once adding a comment that showed where his heart really was: "For that kind of money, I'd expect John Barrymore." Putting aside the troubling image of John Barrymore facing a Smoky Joe Wood fastball, Ruth's profile was soon to become much more famous than any actor's.

Finally Ruth believed that someone was appreciating his value as a ballplayer, not as just another member of Frazee's ensemble cast of players. Under Frazee's ownership, Babe had been assigned his own bodyguard to keep him out of trouble. While some concern may have been justified, it was insulting to the Babe and Kennedy quickly abolished the position. "All I ask of you, Babe, is that you give 100 percent on the field and that you don't embarrass the club off the field. I won't have the Kennedy name associated with any scandalous behavior." The straightforward appeal struck a note with Babe and he responded in kind. "I promise that I won't make you regret the faith you're placing in me, Mr. Kennedy. I can't promise to be an angel, but I'll do my best not to embarrass you or the Red Sox." He began to see Kennedy as a great man, a man with vision and fire, and a man with whom he could deal fairly and squarely. It may not have been a match made in heaven, but it was a hell of a match.

Kennedy's efforts to keep Babe Ruth happy paid immediate dividends for the Red Sox. Other Boston players who had been highly sought after by American League rivals—notably the New York Yankees—decided instead to hitch their wagon to Ruth's ascending star, signing long-term contracts with the Red Sox. Among those who Kennedy was able to re-sign was pitcher Carl Mays, who compiled a record of 80–39 in his next four years in Beantown, including two 25-plus-win seasons. Dutch Leonard also re-signed with the Sox, along with Ernie Shore and Duffy Lewis. It was the continuation of a happy trend—the best players wanted to stay with the Sox or come and play with them.

Yankees owner Ruppert remained persistent, opening his vault to entice the Babe to New York. He practically waved dollar bills in the Babe's face and offered Kennedy almost a quarter of a million dollars in cash and loans as compensation. Kennedy remained resolute. "No deal!" he said. "Ruth is untouchable."

When rumors persisted, Ruth made his own lyrical pitch, and it was an instant hit with Bosox fans. "Start spreadin' the news," he told columnist Danny O'Shaughnessy, "I ain't leavin' today. I don't want no part of that New York, New York. Those Yankee bums lose, so I'm going to stay. I retch at the very thought of it . . . New York, New York. Don't want to wake up in a city that never sleeps. Right here I'm king of the hill, and New York gives me the creeps. That little town blows, I'm sorry to say. . . . I'm gonna make a grander start—and hit—in old Fenway! If I can make it here, I'll make a pile each year. So it's 'Up yours, New York, New York.'"

Frank Sinatra later recorded a popular song about it. They still play it at Fenway after every Red Sox win.

The Red Sox of 1920 were about to become an offensive juggernaut and a pitching powerhouse. Whenever a new signing was announced, morale jumped in the locker room and among the fans. Kennedy headed off a move by the Yankees and signed pitchers Waite Hoyt and Harry Harper, as well as catcher Wally Schang and infielder Mike McNally, to long-term contracts. Later, he also sealed deals with pitchers Bullet Joe Bush and Sam Jones. In the next nine seasons, Hoyt would go 155–96 and pitch in nine World Series. Bush and Jones would go on to pitch in three World Series for the Red Sox. Other key signings followed— notably Deacon Everett Scott and Jumpin' Joe Dugan—as Kennedy loudly declared his determination to not only maintain but also increase the winning ways of the Boston Red Sox. Struggling Herb Pennock was kept in the stable and developed into an ace. Kennedy's masterstroke in keeping Pennock, Jones, Hoyt, and Bush would give the Red Sox stability for years to come. The Yankees' official response was practically apoplectic. Said a spokesperson for the team, "We will not buy a world

Based on his performance with the Yankees, if Babe Ruth had remained in Boston, he probably would have brought the city six more world championships. He probably would have been made honorary mayor, and then the governor would have given him a job, and because of his drinking they probably would have sent him to the Vatican to recover. And he would have gone down the list of lines, and he would have been canonized and sainted, and today we would celebrate St. Babe Ruth Day! St. Ruth, the patron saint of home runs and seven-year-old Scotch. His statue would be in the middle of Kenmore Square, and even the pigeons would be afraid to shit on it.

Meanwhile, New York would have remained small and diminutive, and today the grand city of the United States would be Boston. New York would have been considered almost quaint, and today their fans would be taciturn and timid—not boisterous, arrogant, bloodthirsty, and carnivorous—slinking out of the subway to go to Yankee Stadium. And they would be a little bitter too. Let's see how they handle 80 years of losing! The irony is that New York was basically purchased by the Dutch, and Ruth was basically German, with that same type of beer-drinking, hard-living Teutonic cast. Maybe that's why he ended up there instead of in the puritanical environment of New England, because Ruth was definitely not puritanical.

championship. Please pardon our boasting, but Yankees ownership has convictions."

The Red Sox ignored the whining and kept on signing. Harry Hooper, one-third of what had been called the "greatest outfield ever," was re-signed as well. Although on the downhill side of his brilliant career, Hooper was still a winner. And there was plenty of pop left in his bat too. He was a great outfielder who had been in Frazee's doghouse. He continued to contribute mightily to the Red Sox offense and also offered great defensive skills. He was platooned with Ruth in right field and played there when Babe was pitching. A patient hitter who drew a lot of walks, Hooper was

In 1974, principal Yankees owner George Steinbrenner was convicted of making illegal contributions to Richard Nixon's 1972 reelection campaign. He was later pardoned by Ronald Reagan.

the Red Sox's leadoff man, and with the durable Everett Scott batting second, Ruth's RBI totals soared into the stratosphere. And while the aging Duffy Lewis was allowed to go to the Yanks, Kennedy worked his magic to bring Tris Speaker out of exile in Cleveland. In a blockbuster deal that stunned the baseball world, Kennedy used his magic to perform the coup de grace: he sent seven players, including pitcher Ernie Shore, and $50,000 to Cleveland to reacquire Tris Speaker from the Indians. Cleveland had been on the verge of an American League championship each of the three previous seasons, only to fall short each time. Speaker had slumped to .296 in 1919, his lowest-ever average for a full season. The Cleveland owners felt that a shake-up was in order—something to put them over the top. They thought that unloading the high-salaried, over-the-hill veteran might rejuvenate the team and free up money to purchase other talent.

Predictably, the deal sent shock waves through the American League. Citing "irregularities," the New York Yankees demanded an investigation. Their objections ceased when allegations were made in the press about Yankees tampering with Red Sox players under contract. In 1916 Speaker, like Hooper, had been a third of the "greatest outfield ever." He loved Boston and had never wanted to leave. Only when former owner Joe Lannin threatened to cut his salary did he move on to the Indians. His trade had been a crushing blow to the Red Sox and the fans of New England. Speaker and Cobb were generally acknowledged to be the most complete players in the game. While he had prospered in Cleveland and had been elevated to the position of player/manager partway through the 1919 season, his heart was still in Beantown. The Red Sox offered to make him a manager in Boston as well.

In the off-season, the biggest scandal in baseball history threatened the very foundation of the game. Eight members of the Chicago White Sox were accused of fixing the 1919 World Series. Although a Chicago jury ultimately acquitted them, newly named baseball commissioner Judge Kenesaw Mountain Landis banned the players from baseball forever. Of course, in sophisticated Boston, the very idea of anyone or anything being banned was considered absurd. In the city to the south, the expression "nixed in New York" became a catchphrase for parochialism and narrow-mindedness. Babe Ruth spoke out passionately in defense of Shoeless Joe Jackson, the most prominent of the eight men accused. Ruth had modeled his swing after Jackson's—"His is the perfectest," he said—and felt a kinship with the naive country slugger. He threatened to boycott the season if the ban was not lifted, and he promised to take other American League stars with him.

Bowing to the pressure, the commissioner quickly lifted the ban on Jackson, explaining, "It was obvious from his performance in the World Series that Joe had played to the utmost limit of his abilities." Jackson was thrilled, but, stung by the scandal and fearing a backlash from fans, the tightfisted White Sox hesitated to re-sign their star. Kennedy and the Red Sox quickly jumped in to sign him, giving them yet another potent offensive weapon alongside the Babe. At 30, Jackson was at the peak of his abilities. His batting average the previous year was .382 and his career batting mark to date was a whopping .356. Although he was no Babe Ruth in the power department, he was no Ty Cobb either, and as the ball was livened up, his bat also sprung to life. He and Ruth went on a hitting rampage in 1921 that was to continue through-out the decade of the twenties, until Jackson finally retired after the 1930 season.

As the 1920 season got under way, Boston's populace was absorbed with two things: Babe Ruth and the Sacco and Vanzetti "trial of the century." Einstein visited New York to lecture at Columbia University. Two New York Yankees fans showed up for the event, distant cousins who were convinced that his theory of relativity might explain their family connection. Einstein then moved on to Boston, where thousands of Red Sox fans, mostly Harvard and MIT graduates, filled Fenway Park to hear his theories. Afterward, the great genius confided: "Those Red Sox fans are brilliant, but as for New Yorkers, hoo boy! I asked vun guy vut E equals, and he said 'Another error by the Yankee shortstop?' Verrrry interestink. But dumb."

After all the wheeling and dealing was completed and the dust had settled, the Red Sox lineup, quickly to be dubbed the Boston Brawlers, was usually as follows:

> RF/1B : Harry Hooper
> SS : Everett Scott
> RF : Babe Ruth
> LF : Shoeless Joe Jackson
> CF : Tris Speaker
> 3B/1B : Stuffy McInnis
> 2B : Joe Dugan
> C : Wally Schang

When Ruth pitched, he usually batted at the lower end of the lineup to remove some of the distraction and allow him to con-centrate on pitching. Nevertheless, Ruth the batter, hitting ninth, won countless games for Ruth the pitcher. With Ruth on the mound, the Red Sox moved Harry Hooper to right field, and utility players,

I was at a cocktail party in '69 down at Princeton University and Albert Einstein was there. He came up to this guy sitting on my left and asked him what his IQ was. The guy said it was 160. Einstein said, "Good, I can talk physics with you!" Then he asked me what my IQ was, and I said 120, and he said, "Oh, good, I can talk geography with you." Then he turned to the guy on my right and asked his IQ, and he said it was 86. Einstein scratched his head and finally said, "Go Yankees!"

> "You teach me baseball and I'll teach you relativity. . . . No, we must not. You will learn about relativity faster than I learn baseball."
> —Albert Einstein

including outfielder Shano Collins, took over at first.

The team's defensive prowess rivaled their offensive power. Tris Speaker played the shallowest center field ever and was dubbed "a fifth infielder" by Ruth. Although Ruth's range was limited, he had great defensive instincts, positioned himself well for opposing batters, and never threw to the wrong base.

The Red Sox pitching staff, known as the Boston Stranglers due to the way they choked off opposition runs and killed rallies, looked like this:

Babe Ruth (L)
Carl Mays (R)
Herb Pennock (L)
Sam Jones (R)
Joe Bush (R)
Dutch Leonard (R)
Waite Hoyt (R)

Two years later right-hander Howard Ehmke and others came along, and the Red Sox mound machine just kept on rolling.

Einstein had more than physics equations in that brilliant mind of his: here, Albert regales Bill Lee with another blistering Yankees joke.

It was a lineup conjured up by the baseball gods, and there appeared to be no weaknesses. When Red Sox fans contemplated the fact that many of these stars could have been shipped off to New York or other American League cities, they shuddered.

Before the 1920 season was finished, the lineup would make baseball history. Tris Speaker would have his greatest year at the plate. Shoeless Joe Jackson, thrilled that the inquisition was over, would continue to flirt with .400. And Babe . . . well, Babe was Babe. It was the greatest outfield in the history of the game: Jackson, Speaker, and Ruth. Even when Hooper filled in for Babe while Babe toed the rubber, it was still the greatest outfield in baseball history.

Throaty cries emanated from New York: "Break up the Red Sox!" But these Red Sox had no intention of unraveling any time soon.

All the elements were now in place for a D-Y-N-A-S-T-Y. But other teams had possessed great talent and still managed to lose.

Team chemistry was the key, and the question was asked around Boston: will these stars come together as a team or will it be every man for himself? They needn't have worried.

> "Baseball is dull only to dull minds."
>
> —announcer Red Barber

With a stable starting rotation and Ruth driving in runs in clusters, the Red Sox rebounded from the disastrous 1919 season to win the pennant in 1920 by five games. With his contract worries behind him, Ruth broke loose as a hitter in 1920. The introduction of a livelier ball coincided with his frequent trips from the mound to the outfield, and he went on a hitting rampage that had fans flocking to Fenway and ballparks throughout the American League. He finished the season with an unheard-of 54 homers, more than any other team in the league. Despite the prodigious distances to right field at Fenway Park, Ruth feasted on American League pitchers and there was no park in America—Yellowstone included—that could contain his kind of power. Even when the Red Sox held huge leads, fans stuck around to see Ruth's last at-bat, realizing that they were witnessing history in the making. "It ain't over 'til the fat baby swings," said one sign spotted in the bleachers.

Four teams had actually battled down the stretch for American League honors: the Red Sox, the Indians, the White Sox, and the Yankees. Ultimately the Cleveland Indians, minus Tris Speaker, finished second, a game ahead of the scandal-plagued Chicago White Sox. The Yankees had their destiny in their own hands as they faced the Indians in a late season four-game series that could have carried them to the top of the standings. The two teams battled down to the wire in each hard-fought game, but the same man beat them in each game. Tribe shortstop Ray Chapman went on a tear. Crowding the plate, the one-man wrecking crew led the Indians to four straight wins. He walked eight times in the four games and contributed five key hits, single-handedly eliminating the

Yanks from postseason contention and dropping them to fourth place. Red Sox pitcher Carl Mays suggested that if he were a Yankees pitcher he would have tried to move Chapman back from the plate with some inside fastballs.

The Red Sox had an easy time defeating the National League champion Brooklyn Dodgers, winning the World Series in seven games. When someone gave the celebrating Ruth news that the League of Nations had just been formed, Ruth replied: "When they finish their pennant drive, we'll lick them too!" After the season, Ruth was not only the talk of New England but also the toast of baseball. Fifty-four homers were unheard of, and his name was fast becoming a household word.

But Ruth was only one arrow in the Red Sox quill, albeit the most lethal one. Joe Jackson, back from banishment, batted .382, third best in the AL. Tris Speaker returned to his old form, batting .388, second only to George Sisler's .407. Ruth and Speaker finished one-two in various offensive categories. Ruth led the league in walks with 148, and Speaker was second with 97. Ruth led in runs scored with 158, and Speaker added 137. Ruth led in on-base percentage with .530, and Speaker was second with .483. Jackson led in triples with 20 and Speaker in doubles with 50. Both had more than 200 hits. With Babe's astounding .847 slugging mark leading the way, all three outfielders finished in the top four in that category. They also finished in the top four in total bases.

Ruth's hitting heroics transformed the game and led other teams, including the Yankees, to seek out and sign power hitters of their own. Traditional hitters such as Ty Cobb, Harry Heilmann, and Tris Speaker were no longer the only signing priority around the league. Owners scouted players like Hack Wilson, Al Simmons, Mel Ott, Chuck Klein, Goose Goslin, and Jimmie Foxx, players who could hit for power as well as for average. Singles and doubles hitters were no longer the glamour boys of baseball.

In 1921, the Red Sox, with assistance from the city of Boston, completely redesigned Fenway Park, replacing the Wall in left with a more conventional one and extending the home-run distance to a more challenging 340 feet. The bleachers were extended all the way to the left-field foul pole and an extra deck was added, increasing capacity to 50,000. The 37-foot Wall was then transferred to right field and placed precisely 315 feet from home plate, a mirror image of what it had been the previous year. When the Babe first saw the changes after returning from an extended road trip, he was delighted.

"I could bunt one over that thing!" he quipped.

Over the next few seasons, Ruth proceeded to hit homers in unheard-of numbers, and his pitching never faltered, despite the double duty. Occasionally, on the day before a start, the manager limited him to pinch-hitting duties or played him at first, to save wear and tear on his precious arm. More than once in key games, he provided both the pitching and the offense for the Red Sox. Fans were beginning to call him a one-man team.

Babe's all-out assault on baseball continued throughout the '21 season. American League pitchers were at a loss as to how to get him out. Albert Einstein, who had become a good friend of Ruth's, won the Nobel Prize that year, but the Babe won almost everything else, including the home-run and RBI titles.

The decade of the twenties belonged to the Boston Red Sox. They won the American League flag and the World Series every year in that decade—and usually convincingly. Sure, there were other great teams and lots of great players; the Tigers had Ty Cobb, some would argue the most dominating of them all, and the National League featured such stars as Rogers Hornsby and Bill Terry. The difference was that the Red Sox had it all. They won with pitching and they won with hitting and they won with defense.

The Babe hit well on the road, and his flair for headlines pushed him to excel in big-market media centers, especially New

York. In fact, New York gradually became his favorite road city, and the fans there developed a kind of love-hate relationship with the big guy. The Yankees tried repeatedly to entice him away from the Red Sox, but to no avail. Ruth was Boston and Boston was Ruth, although he loved to rib the Boston fans and media with the boast, "If I played in New York, they'd name a candy bar after me! Some kind of bar, at least."

In Boston, they could well have named booze after him. Babe's beer, Babe's bourbon, Ruth's rum, George's gin—he drank them all. (Babe's root beer failed to take off as expected.) Sometimes his binges were of historical significance. He often spent time at Boston's famous Parker House. One evening, while drinking in his room, the Babe decided he wanted some female companionship. He called room service and drunkenly demanded that a prostitute be sent up immediately. Within five minutes a young Vietnamese busboy named Ho Chi Minh arrived at his door with a tray heaped high with more drinks. "Who in hell are you?" demanded the Babe. "You ask for Ho. I am Ho!" replied the confused servant. Babe was furious at the mistake and a terrible fight ensued. Ruth finally picked up the tray and crashed it down on the busboy's head, killing him instantly. In this era of the "Red scare," almost any foreigner was deemed a radical, and a short trial—the Ho Chi Minh Trial—absolved Babe of any blame in the incident. The tray used to kill the Vietnamese radical is still on display in the lobby of the hotel, with an appropriately engraved plaque attached. The plaque reads: The Ho Chi Minh Tray. Back in Vietnam, newspapers reported that an expatriate had been killed by some "big ugly gorilla." Guerrilla warfare was hence banned forever in southeast Asia.

The Red Sox won the pennant in 1921 and again in 1922, and each year they overpowered the New York Giants to capture the World Series. Kennedy offered Ruth a new three-year deal worth $150,000. King Tut's tomb was discovered that same year, and Boston writer Peter O'Gammons suggested that the Babe be mummified when he died. "Why wait," said the Babe, and took another shot of Scotch. Even with the additional seating, Fenway Park was much too small to house the hordes of baseball fans that wanted to see the Babe and his playmates. There was talk of a brand-new ballpark, and two rival factions polarized the community. Bumper stickers saying SAVE FENWAY appeared on automobiles. DEMOLISH FENWAY stickers appeared on signposts. The Massachusetts state legislature worked feverishly to come up with a plan of action to resolve the impasse. They still meet every Tuesday.

Meanwhile in New York, the Ruth-less Yankees continued to struggle. Yankee Stadium was opened on April 18, 1923. As luck would have it, the Red Sox were playing the Yankees that day and Ruth ruined the grand opening by belting a three-run homer in the top of the fourth to carry the visitors to a 4–1 win. The new Yankees home was dubbed the House That Wrath Built, because New Yorkers were so consumed by jealousy and hatred of the city of Boston and its beautiful Fenway Park. The Red Sox won the '23 American League flag and once again knocked the National League champion New York Giants off their beanstalk.

In the Big Apple, a clean-cut young Yankees fan named Donaldo Gambino decided that it was time to act. As head of a local boys club known as the Cozy Nostrils, he and his rascally little friends tried to think of a way to get Babe Ruth traded to New York. Their first move was to go to a gypsy mystic in Brooklyn and ask her to use her powers to put a spell on Ruth. Amused by the cute little street urchins, the mystic promised to use her supernatural powers to put Ruth into a prolonged slump until he saw the light and moved to New York. However, this "curse on the Bambino" did not work, and the frustrated Gambino resorted to more sinister methods.

He began by consulting his priest. "Can you imagine if we had Ruth and Lou Gehrig in the same lineup?" said Donaldo. "God, Father, why it would be a regular Murderer's Incorporated."

"Murderer's Row," the father corrected. "I suggest that you make Joe Kennedy an offer he can't refuse."

Gambino took his advice, sending a not-so-subtle message to Kennedy early one morning. Kennedy was lying in bed with his wife and woke up screaming next to a bloody horse's head. He was shaken but still not stirred to action. His wife was philosophical about the threat: "I've been waking up next to a horse's ass for years," she joked. "This makes a nice change." Even Joe didn't seem worried about the thinly veiled threat. "Based on what I see of the Yankees lineup, I doubt if these guys could find a reliable hit man in the whole city of New York." Frustrated once again, Gambino turned to a life of crime, and the entire crime-infested city of New York still bears the "curse of the Gambino."

The Red Sox won their fifth straight world championship in 1924, the same year that J. Edgar Hoover became head of the scandal-ridden FBI. Hoover was secretly asked by the Yankees to investigate the Red Sox organization from top to bottom, starting with Babe Ruth. Since Hoover saw "Reds" everywhere anyway, he was quite willing to look for them in Boston (and Cincinnati, too). Hoover felt that any man with a sissy name like Babe Ruth must be some kind of cross-dressing pervert. Later that night, he slipped into his high heels and evening gown and decided to pay a visit to this Ruth guy. . . . The next day, nursing a black eye and a broken nose, and with a terrible run in his nylons, Hoover started a file on George Herman Ruth.

A new hero emerged in New York in 1925 as well. His name was Lou Gehrig and, although he wasn't yet Babe Ruth, he did hit 20 homers, and it looked like he might stick around for a while if he could stay healthy. The Yankees organization surrounded the Columbia University graduate with a decent supporting cast, and the 1925 Yankees finished the season a half game behind the Red Sox. The Scopes monkey trial was receiving national attention, and Yankees fans protested that it was unfair to prosecute primates because they were just "poor dumb creatures." Prosecutor William Jennings Bryan visited Yankee Stadium and revised his views on evolution. "Based on what I saw there, Clarence," said Bryan to defender Clarence Darrow, "it appears there might be something to this theory of man evolving from the apes after all." The Red Sox rallied to capture the pennant on the final day of the season and swept the World Series against the National League's Pittsburgh Pirates.

The Sox returned to their dominating ways in 1926, coasting to the pennant and then plucking the St. Louis Cardinals 4–0 in the World Series. The word *dynasty* was no longer just idle talk. There were cries of "Break up the Red Sox!" and some disgruntled New Yorkers said that cheering for the Red Sox was "about as exciting as rooting for U.S. Steel."

Early in 1927, Red Sox fortunes appeared ready to drop. Their lineup was weakened by retirements and aging stars. Meanwhile, the Yankees were coming on like gangbusters. Predictably, by midseason the New York newspapers were starting to call the '27 Yankees the greatest team ever assembled, even though it was only early May. Even Bostonians, however, were forced to admit that their lineup was impressive. Led by Lou Gehrig, the Yanks became known as Murderer's Row and featured Combs, Meusel, Lazzeri, and Koenig.

Mount Rushmore was dedicated to honor great Americans, and many felt that Babe Ruth's image should have been carved as well. "We'd need Everest to accomplish that," said the artist. Charles Lindbergh flew solo from New York to Paris, and the Holland Tunnel opened connecting New York and New Jersey, prompting Babe Ruth to quip: "People will go to any lengths to get out of this town." Calvin Coolidge uttered his famous words, "I chose not to run," a cry that was quickly taken up by Yankees base runners when facing the Red Sox pitchers. Also in 1927, Babe starred in a movie called *Babe Comes Home*. According to his long-suffering wife, it was pure fiction.

Ruth and Gehrig battled all season long for the home-run crown. Going into the dog days of August, it was still a horse race. In September, however, the Babe galloped past the Iron Horse, pounding out 18 home runs in that month alone. He finished with the unheard-of total of 60 homers while Gehrig finished second with 47. Between the two, they hit one-quarter of all the home runs hit in the AL that year. Yankees fans could only dream of what might have been if Ruth and Gehrig had played together on the same team.

When the Yankees came to town in late June for a key series, the Red Sox publicity director dressed Ruth up in a Paul Revere outfit and sent him on horseback down Massachusetts Avenue yelling, "The Yankees are coming, the Yankees are coming." But hype was scarcely needed to bring fans to the ballpark to watch the mighty Red Sox. Every game was a sellout and the Fenway coffers were bulging.

The 1927 Yankees were a good match for the Red Sox in power, but Boston possessed more balance and better pitching. Their airtight defense choked off opposition runs with ease. In head-to-head battle that year, the Red Sox beat the Yankees in every game and, with a little help from the surging Philadelphia Athletics, edged them out by a single game. The margin of victory was provided by Waite Hoyt, one of the players the Yankees had attempted to steal from the Red Sox a few years earlier. Hoyt won a league-leading 22 games for the Sox that year and would almost certainly have made the difference in leading the Yankees to their first pennant. But it was not to be. On the final day of the season, a doubleheader, Hoyt won the first game, 3–2, and with 50,000 screaming Fenway fans on hand, Babe Ruth pitched the second game, winning 4–0 on the margin of his own grand-slam homer in the bottom of the ninth.

Over the next few years, Ruth's supporting cast entered and exited, but the Red Sox continued to win, always seeming to snatch victory from the jaws of the Yankees in key series late in the summer. The fact that the Yankees of this era were very good teams, and in some ways stronger on paper than the Red Sox, made their losing even tougher for the New York fans. It always seemed to be Babe Ruth who provided the heroics for the Red Sox, and Ruth always seemed to best the New York hero Gehrig. Yankees fans took to wearing bags over their heads when the Red Sox came to town; some even donned two bags "in case the first one falls off."

Medical history was made in the late twenties when Englishman Alexander Fleming discovered penicillin. Also in the late twenties, Ruth hit his peak as a power hitter with totals of 47, 60, 54, and 46. The two facts are believed to be unrelated, but predictably, reports emanated from New York that in Ruth's case penicillin should be classified as a "performance-enhancing drug."

In 1929, the Yankees again succumbed to a late-September surge by the Bosox. It proved to be too much for some New Yorkers. As construction got under way on the pride of New York, the Empire State Building, queues of suicidal Yankees fans began to form at the site. Due to the plummeting New York Stock Exchange, however, the construction of the Empire State Building stopped at the sixth floor. Fearing only serious injury instead of death, Yankees fans instead formed queues to jump off the Brooklyn Bridge. Fights broke out between suicidal stock traders and suicidal Yankees fans for the "best jumping spot." Meanwhile in Boston, the state legislature had renamed the Bay State the Babe State, and the new Babe State Building was completed and heralded as the tallest structure in America. Plans to shoot the movie *King Kong* in New York were scrapped, and it was filmed in Boston instead.

The stock market finally crashed on Black Tuesday. Wall Street became a series of vacant lots. The Boston Stock Exchange soon became the financial center of America. Located in a building across the street from the Green Monster, it was immediately dubbed The Wall Street. Bo-stocks, as they came to be known, were the standard for the financial world.

The New York Yankees were such a bland and nondescript group that the owners decided to put numbers on the back of their uniforms so that fans would know who was messing up. Yankees players demanded that numbers also be put on the backs of the obnoxious New York fans so that they could identify them after the game. Ripley's "Believe It or Not" made its first appearance in newspapers in '29. For a brief period, the Yankees used the phrase as a rallying cry, but it failed to catch on.

Boston was now America's center of banking and commerce as well as of the retail trade, the publishing business, and, as always, culture and higher education. Rumors were rampant that soon even the Statue of Liberty would be moved from New York Harbor to Boston Harbor. The argument was made that Boston was a far more welcoming environment for the "huddled masses yearning to breathe free." *Globe* columnist Danny O'Shaughnessy quipped that Yankee Stadium would continue to be the refuge for "muddled asses willing to pay the fee."

Ernest Hemingway's classic *A Farewell to Arms* was published. Unsophisticated New Yorkers refused to buy it, believing it to be yet another depressing tale about the state of the Yankees pitching staff.

Babe Ruth was doing wonders for New England tourism. Few towns from Maine to New Hampshire didn't boast at least one house with a plaque that read: The Babe slept here. The idea caught on and Quincy, Massachusetts, ice cream entrepreneur Howard Johnson spawned a chain of popular hotels throughout the region. Their motto was: You'll sleep like a babe at Babe's.

In 1930, Joe Kennedy was a happy man. He had forecast the Depression and had taken advantage of his business smarts to "sell short." He advised his friend Ruth to do the same. At first Ruth was skeptical. "The only depression I know is the one my ass makes when I sit on the couch," he quipped. But he ultimately

New York City five years after the Babe decided to stay in Boston.

took Kennedy's advice and made a million dollars in two years. Kennedy's wealth quickly grew into millions of dollars, and he no longer needed to participate in shady enterprises. He spent money lavishly on his beloved Red Sox, acquiring Jimmie Foxx from the Philadelphia Athletics. Ruth and Foxx went on to give the Red Sox the biggest one-two power punch in the history of the game. The Beast and the Babe took Boston by storm. Foxx immediately began an assault on Babe's home-run record of 60. The two men battled throughout the season before the younger Foxx finally pulled ahead for good. In the end, he finished with 58 homers, but observers estimated that he would have hit another 10 if the Green Monster had been left where it was. Foxx and Ruth were often seen out on the town; reports of this were hushed up by the Boston ownership. Their drinking and carousing inspired the nicknames Double X and Triple X.

The thirties were to be a time of change for the Red Sox, as Babe's star was showing signs of fading. Nevertheless, Kennedy re-signed him for $160,000 over three years. Ruth promptly won the home-run title again with 49 and out-slugged everyone in baseball with a .732 mark. In 1931, he again topped the league in slugging but shared the home-run title with Gehrig, who hit 46.

In 1933, sensing that Prohibition would soon be repealed, the ingenious Kennedy imported Haig & Haig and Dewar's as "medicines" and kept them in a warehouse in anticipation. Some doctors even started to pre-scribe whiskey for their lucky patients. They called the alco-holic medications "the cures of the Bambino." Right on cue, Pro-

> "A baseball club is part of the chemistry of the city. A game isn't just an athletic contest. It's a picnic, a kind of town meeting."
>
> —Michael Burke

hibition ended in December and Kennedy was well stocked with liquid gold. To celebrate, Babe Ruth himself dumped a truckload of tea in Boston Harbor to symbolize the end of enforced teetotaling.

Mere days after the repeal of Prohibition, Joe Kennedy, wanting to enter the political arena, finally sold the Red Sox to a wealthy young southerner—by way of Detroit and New York—named Thomas Yawkey. Changes loomed on the horizon. Yawkey idolized Ruth, and the two were frequent drinking companions. Despite his age, Ruth could still occasionally get around on a fastball and drive it to the deepest reaches of the right-field bleachers at Fenway. Most of all, the Babe was still a winner, and he was still a huge draw wherever he played, especially in New York, where he had enjoyed some of his most dramatic moments. In the "Zoo Built by Lou," as the new Yankee Stadium was known by visiting players, Babe's home-run battles with Gehrig had cap-tured the imaginations of both cities and the entire nation. How-ever, Yankee Stadium was a house with a reputation that was ill—if not a house of ill repute.

"You mix two jiggers of Scotch to one jigger of Metrecal. So far I've lost five pounds and my driver's license."
—Rocky Bridges, on his diet

"Always carry a flagon of whiskey in case of snakebite, and furthermore, always carry a small snake."
—W. C. Fields

There was no doubt that Babe's biggest rival was only a few hundred miles down the road in New York. Gehrig and Ruth were the two biggest power hitters in the American League, and they battled each other year after year for league hitting honors.

Gehrig and Ruth had tied for the league lead in homers in 1931, but Lou had the edge in RBIs with 184. Year after year, the rivalry seemed to drive both athletes to new heights of achievement. In 10 seasons of head-to-head competition—from Gehrig's first full season with the Yankees in 1925 until Ruth's last season with the Red Sox in 1934—Ruth topped him in homers nine times; Lou bested Babe in RBIs in '27, '28, '30, '31, '32, '33, and '34. Only in 1931, when Babe was all but a spent force, did the younger Gehrig assume the home-run mantle, hitting 49 round-trippers to the Babe's positively puny—by his standards anyway—22.

The rivalry had been great for baseball, and fans flocked to Fenway Park and Yankee Stadium to see the two sluggers duke it out. New York and Boston drew huge crowds throughout the league, and attendance records were broken in seven consecutive years. Although a mutual respect existed between the flamboyant Babe and the reserved Gehrig, there was nothing of the sort between fans of the two teams. Beantown or the Bronx, it didn't matter; all-out war broke out every time the two teams met.

Coincidentally, Ruth's final season was the same year that Alcoholics Anonymous was founded. "Thank God I missed it," said the Babe. The years of Red Sox championships had also inspired the creation of a game called Monopoly. And Social Security was introduced to placate the dying city of New York.

Since Ruth's arrival in 1914, the Red Sox had won 10 pennants and seven World Series. He was now well past his prime and there were other hitters who were about to surpass him. The Red Sox had their eye on a brash young prospect from southern California, who was as skinny as Babe was porky. Word was, the cocky guy they called the "Kid" could hit pretty well. FIRST THE BABE, NOW THE KID headlined Leigh O'Montville's article in the *Boston Globe.*

Ruth had revolutionized the game when he turned his attention from pitching to hitting, and he set long-ball records that would never be approached. The new 62,000-seat Fenway Park, which managed to keep the same playing-field dimensions, was known as the Babe's Cradle. The nickname "the House that Ruth helped to rebuild with help from Boston city council and a bipartisan committee of the state of Massachusetts Legislature" failed to catch on with fans.

Gehrig did succeed in having a candy bar—Lou's Chews—named after him. Not to be outdone, the Boston Baked Bean Emporium came out with a new product known as Babe's Baked Beans. It became a popular New England delicacy that featured a dash of beer during the baking process. The joke around Boston was that Babe's Beans were far more potent than Lou's Chews.

Babe loved dogs, especially racing dogs, and he developed a stable of champions. In his column, Danny O'Shaughnessy referred to them as the "curs of the Bambino."

Ruth hit his home runs in a ballpark that did no favors for left-handed power hitters. The question was often asked: what would the Babe have done in New York, with its cozy right-field porch? Occasional rumors of a trade of Gehrig for Ruth surfaced but were quickly denied by both franchises.

■ ■ ■

Meanwhile, the Yankees franchise continued to flounder as year after year the team came out second best to the Red Sox. The Red Sox made money hand over fist, while the Yankees struggled to meet payroll. O'Shaughnessy called this phenomenon the "purse of the Bambino," since only the Babe was able to fill both Fenway and Yankee Stadium. New York writers became very cynical, and their reportage was full of hatred, self-loathing, and sarcasm. Later, when young Joe DiMaggio arrived from San Francisco, the New York writers criticized his every move on and off the field, often delving into his private

The curs of the Bambino.

life. Conversely, Ted Williams became the darling of the Boston media, and he flourished in the positive, upbeat, and supportive environment. Ted was so appreciative of their noble behavior that he dubbed them "the knights of the typewriter" and addressed each one as "sir."

With his skills finally beginning to wane, Ruth made the decision to retire following the 1934 season. His last year with the Red Sox proved to be a poignant farewell to baseball. Every city in the American League had a Babe Ruth Day. Some were extravagant, some subdued, but all paid fitting tribute to his impact on the game. The two most touching were in New York and, of course, Boston. In New York, where baseball talent was still appreciated by the pennant-starved fans, the Babe got standing ovations every time he came to the plate throughout the season. On August 13, the Red Sox and the Yankees met at the Stadium for the last time. Before the game, the Babe and his archrival Lou Gehrig shook hands during an emotional ceremony that had many in the crowd in tears. Ruth had always loved playing in New York, and his offensive statistics there were the stuff of legend. Watching Ruth and Gehrig was like

The Bambino and the Splendid Splinter: Bosox baseball would never be the same.

watching two sides of the same coin. Ruth was uneducated, brash, and loud; Gehrig was college-educated, quiet, and reserved. But both were great hitters.

In the winter of 1935, Ruth was immediately named vice president and honorary batting instructor for the Red Sox, a position he continued to hold for the next 10 years. Ted Williams gave Babe credit for inspiring him to reach even greater hitting goals.

■ ■ ■

Babe Ruth and Joe Kennedy had become more than owner and player, they were fast friends. Throughout his career and beyond, Ruth was a frequent visitor at the Kennedys' cottage retreat in Hyannisport on Cape Cod. He grew close to Joe and his wife, Rose, and all the Kennedy kids, but especially Joe Jr. and Jack. While chronologically Ruth was more a contemporary of the father than the sons, the society pages of the *Boston Globe* sometimes referred to the man-child as the "other Kennedy child, the Babe of the family." It was an unlikely friendship. The Kennedys were favored with poise, prestige, and privilege; Ruth was full of piss and vinegar. This large, relaxed, and welcoming Catholic family was completely alien to Ruth's experience as a virtual orphan, abandoned by his parents. The Kennedys were Harvard-educated; Ruth, labeled "an incorrigible," had attended St. Mary's Industrial School for Boys in Baltimore, a combination reform school and orphanage.

Some members of Boston's upper echelon looked askance at the friendship between the womanizing, gluttonous, heavy-drinking Ruth and America's "royal family." "The socially adept meets the socially inept," one society-page columnist sniffed, before adding, "The only thing refined about Ruth is the high-octane whiskey he drinks." In truth, the only things the Kennedys and the Babe had in common were Catholicism, charisma, and a love—no, a lust—for life. Babe played touch football on the lawn with the boys and girls, went sailing with them, and as the boys came of age, shared drinks with them. This was the middle of Prohibition and Ruth knew that drinks—and good-quality drinks—were always available in Kennedy's home. That fact alone was enough to keep him coming back.

He used to enjoy talking about politics with the teenaged John Kennedy, a boy wise beyond his years. One day Ruth was flexing his powerful arm muscles and complaining that his salary was not high enough, saying he wanted a raise or he'd go play baseball in Cuba. "In Cuba they would appreciate muscles like mine." Young Jack replied: "Let me say this about that, Babe. Ask not what the Red Sox can do for you, ask rather what you can do for the Red Sox." Kennedy later paraphrased his inspirational advice and used it to great advantage. Babe realized he was being selfish, and the Cuban muscle crisis was avoided.

With the birth of Teddy Kennedy in 1932, Babe was now a favorite "uncle" to nine Kennedy children—Joe Jr., John, Rosemary, Eunice, Patricia, Robert, Kathleen, Jean, and Edward. "Enough to field a pretty good ball team," Ruth joked. Chubby Teddy followed Ruth around like a baby duckling waddling after its mother. He would sit on Babe's lap, drinking from his baby bottle while Babe enjoyed a cold beer and told him long stories of his exploits on and off the field. Teddy's first full sentence was, "Me wanna be like Babe." His parents, as much as they loved Ruth, shuddered at the thought. Joe turned to Rose in bed that night and said prophetically, "I love him as much as you do, but I worry about his influence on the boys. Mark my words, if any of them ever go astray later in life, look for the Babe to be involved somehow."

In 1937, when Joe Kennedy had become ambassador to Britain, the headline writers had a field day with the unlikely friendship between the two men:

AMBASSADOR HOSTS SULTAN OF SWAT
MAHARAJAH OF MASH MEETS WITH
   AMBASSADOR KENNEDY
KENNEDY COURTS KING OF CLOUT
POWER SUMMIT IN HYANNISPORT

A Republican newspaper ran a picture of the two with the caption: Maniac Diplomat Hosts Dipsomaniac: former bootlegger and best customer socialize.

When Joe Jr. and Jack ran for public office, Babe Ruth was always there to make stump speeches on their behalf, and when Joe was elected president of the United States in 1944, Babe was made honorary Secretary of Fitness, to the delight and general amusement of the American public. When Babe visited the president at the White House, the svelte young leader and the potbellied athlete smoked cigars and talked about old times on Cape Cod. Eight years later, after Joe's second term in office had ended, Babe was also instrumental in getting young Jack elected to Congress. "It never hurts your image to be seen with the Babe," said the appreciative Kennedy. Kennedy's campaign team wanted Ruth to jump out of a cake and sing happy birthday to the candidate, but he drew the line at that.

Ruth had become Mr. Boston. Beloved throughout New England, he would forever be associated with the city that had been so loyal to him. A statue of Ruth was erected in Kenmore Square. It depicted the Babe swinging a bat while standing atop a pitcher's mound, thus recognizing and honoring his two-dimensional talent. When the Hall of Fame was opened in 1939, Babe Ruth and Joe Jackson were among the first inductees.

In 1940 Babe Ruth ran for election as the mayor of Boston. He had learned a lot about politics from his mentor and friend Joe Kennedy, and with his charm and disarming personality, he was a natural. His platform was a simple one. If elected, he promised to make Boston the Athens of America. "We already have the ath-hole of America in New York," he quipped, "so we might as well have the real thing here in Massachusetts." His campaign slogan was "Ruth, Justice, and the American Way." He won by a landslide.

Aside from the odd cold beer on a hot afternoon, Babe had given up drinking three years earlier and worked out with weights on a regular basis.

In New York, they continue to this day to speak of the great Bambino, and in that city fans have become so cynical and gun-shy that even a huge late-season lead fails to bring comfort. Things got so bad in Gotham that for three years, from 1940 to 1942, the Yankees dropped out of the majors and became one of the Triple A affiliates of the Red Sox. They were an above-average minor league franchise, finishing second in the respected minor league circuit all three years behind the Lowell Pressure, the other Bosox affiliate.

In the fifties a play titled *Damn Red Sox* (based on the novel *The Year the Yankees Won the Pennant*) opened on New York's Broadway with the expectation that if it did well it would make it to the big time in Boston. "Those small-town New York audi-ences may lack sophistication," said the director, "but after watching the Yankees all these years, they know a good farce when they see one." The story involves a middle-aged man who sells his soul to the devil in exchange for the Yankees winning a pennant. Audiences in both cities laughed like hell at the absurd-ity of the Yankees winning a pennant.

■ ■ ■

When Ted Williams arrived on the scene in 1939, he continued the tradition of great-hitting, left-handed outfielders that would continue almost uninterrupted—through Carl Yastrzemski and others—down to the present day. Ruth and Williams discussed hitting by the hour. Although Ted's analysis of the science of hitting was lost on Babe, who hit on instinct, the two formed a close bond, and Ted quizzed Babe like a cub reporter with too much caffeine. Later that year, Harvard University, at the urging of the Kennedy family, bestowed an honorary degree on the Babe: Doctor of Homerology. Although originally a joke, a freshman history course based on Babe's life was introduced in 1940. Bob O'Ryan of the *Globe* called it "the course of the Bambino."

At this writing, the Red Sox now have 37 World Series titles. Meanwhile, in New York they are still waiting for their first World Series championship since entering the American League in 1903. It is the longest drought of any professional sports team in the history of the world.

In 1986 the New York Mets finally came close, leading the Series three games to two and holding a lead in the ninth inning of Game 6. The fans were traumatized by the years of futility, and negativity is the hallmark of this provincial northeastern city. Flush with success, Boston fans sported bumper stickers saying NEW YORK: CHAMPAGNE COOLING SINCE 1903. Fuhgeddaboudit.

■ ■ ■

In 1956, after four productive terms as mayor, Ruth retired from public office and went into retirement. He served as honorary batting instructor for the Sox, but it was not enough for Babe. Inactivity was not his cup of tea, and soon he became extremely ill and was under the constant care of a full-time nurse, who was quickly dubbed by Danny O'Shaughnessy "the nurse of the Bambino." In an emotional scene at Fenway Park, Ruth said good-bye to Boston and all of New England. Boston fans knew that they would never see his like again. He had brought glory to the city, the state, and the entire region, and he made Boston the baseball center of the nation and the world. The state song of Massachusetts was changed to "I Got You, Babe."

When Babe died on August 16, 1958, the entire city of Boston was in mourning for a solid month. His funeral parade through downtown Boston was watched by tens of thousands of fans lining the streets. His funeral car was a black Cadillac. In his poignant farewell in the *Globe,* columnist Will McDonough called it "the hearse of the Bambino."

Babe's No. 60 (he was given that number in the midtwenties) was retired, the first player ever honored in that way by the Red

The nurse of the Bambino.

Sox. In 1970, Route 128, which runs around the circumference of the city, was renamed Route 60 in Ruth's honor. Bostonians just call it the Babe Route.

In poor, downtrodden, dispirited New York, the drought of world championships continues to this very day. There—and *only* there—it is called "the curse of the Bambino."

The hearse of the Bambino.

CHAPTER 4

Führer Furor at Fenway!

*"Adolf may have been the greatest Hitler
who ever lived, but Ted was the greatest hitter! War and baseball cannot coexist! War is
about borders and baseball is without borders. I say tear down all defenses! Ted
Williams would have been the ideal secretary
of defense. Ted would destroy all defenses
just like he tore down de fences when he
destroyed the Boudreau Shift. Adolf Hitler
would have been no match for Ted Williams."*
—Chairman Lee

In 1941, the young Red Sox star Ted Williams had just finished his third and greatest season, one of the very best that base-ball has ever witnessed. The Boston slugger had hit 37 homers, driven in 145 runs, and, most astonishing of all, had batted .406, the first to do so since National Leaguer Bill Terry turned the trick in 1930 and the last hitter ever to reach this plateau. In December of that same year, the Japanese bombed Pearl Harbor, drawing the United States into World War II. As the 1942 season got under way, there were enormous pressures on Williams to enlist in the armed forces, despite the fact that he had been granted a perfectly legit-imate deferment as sole support for his mother. Although he played the entire '42 season, winning the Triple Crown in the process, he signed up for naval aviation early in the campaign. The next few years he would be doffing his Red Sox uniform and donning an armed services uniform.

Ted left for war as the best hitter in baseball. Eventually 5,400 of the 5,800 players who were in pro baseball at the time of Pearl Harbor enlisted and served their country.[1] The ballplayers who remained—with few exceptions—were major leaguers in name only. Most were either too old for military service or, as in the extreme case of one-armed Pete Gray, deemed ineligible to serve because of physical challenges of one sort or another.

When he finally and triumphantly returned from his tour of duty in 1946, Ted picked up where he had left off, powering 38 homers, driving in 123 runs, and batting .342. He was still the best

"Let them try that damned Boudreau Shift on me now!"

"I can't conceive of either team winning a single game."

—writer Warren Brown,
speaking of the
1945 World Series between
the Cubs and the Tigers

Scant days after the Japanese attack on Pearl Harbor, baseball commissioner Kenesaw Mountain Landis approached President Roosevelt and asked him if he wanted Major League Baseball to cease operations during the war. Roosevelt's answer was an emphatic "No!" The president gave the game the green light to continue and even encouraged Landis to schedule more night games so that shift workers could watch the great American pastime. More than ever, playing baseball was equated with patriotism and freedom.

Roosevelt loved baseball and had coached a team in 1900. He attended numerous Washington Senators games in the nation's capital between 1933 and 1941 and still holds the record for the most ceremonial first pitches thrown out by a sitting president.

hitter in baseball. But the fact that he lost those years has been the subject of discussion and conjecture ever since. No one will ever know what might have been accomplished if those years had been restored to Williams and the other men who fought for freedom in World War II, but Ted did not like that kind of talk, proudly declaring that he did not regret one minute of his service to the United States.

While Ted was in his first major league season in 1939, Moe Berg was in his last. It had been a lackluster 15-year career that saw the journeyman catcher bat a modest .243 and manage a meager six homers while playing for the Brooklyn Dodgers, the Chicago White Sox, the Cleveland Indians, the Boston Red Sox, and the Washington Senators. Berg owned a degree in Romance languages from Princeton, and it is tough to think of any practical use he could

One fact is indisputable: Ted Williams was just hitting his prime as a hitter when he enlisted. He was coming off a .400 season followed by a Triple Crown performance. Modest estimates of his home-run totals during those three years and the additional two years lost when Ted was later sent to Korea are in excess of 700 home runs, more than three thousand hits, and untold numbers of additional RBIs. Henry Aaron feels that he would have eclipsed Ruth's home-run total of 714. In *Ted Williams: The Pursuit of Perfection* by Jim Prime and Bill Nowlin, Keith Woolner created a projection for the five years missed to military service.[2] The 1943–45 projections were based on Williams' actual stats up to that point in his career, and the figures for 1952–53, when he was in Korea, were based on actual stats plus the projections for 1943–45.

His findings are as follows:

G = Games
AB = At-bats
R = Runs
H = Hits
HR = Home runs
RBI = Runs batted in
BB = Bases on balls
AVG = Batting average
OBP = On-base percentage
SLG = Slugging percentage

G	AB	R	H	HR	RBI	BB	AVG	OBP	SLG
2,969	10,264	2,492	3,553	701*	2,401	2,757	.346	.485	.635

*One has to believe that if Ted had been within striking distance of Ruth's record 714 at the end of the 1960 campaign, he would have played another season to set the new standard. Perhaps more important, his impact on the fortunes of the talented young Red Sox could have been enormous during those lost years.

make of that as a catcher. He also held a law degree from Columbia University, which conceivably may have helped him in disputing umpires' calls.

Berg played in just 14 games in 1939 and collected only nine

> "We're supposed to be perfect our first day on the job and then show constant improvement."
>
> —Ed Vargo, umpire

hits, one of which was a homer. But he had other duties. Aside from being a spare catcher, he was also the bullpen catcher. More important, he was manager Joe Cronin's assistant in all but official title and acted as a liaison between Cronin and the pitching staff. Cronin had asked Berg to take rookie Ted Williams under his wing and tutor him in the fine points of being a major leaguer.

Their first meeting at batting practice reflected their distinct personalities, as Ted went to the plate without his baseball cap, his unruly hair sticking out in all directions. "What's the matter, Kid, don't they make hats where you come from?" said the veteran. Williams responded with the cockiness that one would expect from Terrible Ted: "If that's all it takes to make the big leagues—here!" And he took his cap from his back pocket and defiantly jammed it onto his head. Despite their differences in age, attitude, and ability, the two hit it off immediately. "I think he liked my young, enthusiastic approach to it all," said Williams.[3]

Of course it has now been well documented that Berg had even more wide-ranging duties. By narrow definition, probably all catchers are spies, but Berg was a real Spy, with a capital *S*. His other life was one of subterfuge and intrigue and espionage. He was a man who called the president "Franklin," a man Winston Churchill later referred to cryptically as "the catcher." He never made the Hall of Fame, although, interestingly, he was the catcher in the very first Hall of Fame game when it opened its doors in

1939. His baseball card and uniform are on exhibit at the CIA's Exhibit Center in Virginia.

Berg accompanied Babe Ruth and others on barnstorming tours of Japan and used a small movie camera to document various installations for later use by Jimmy Doolittle and his bombers. He eventually worked for the Office of Strategic Services, a precursor of today's CIA. Among other covert missions, he was asked to determine the capabilities of Germany's atomic bomb initiative. In short, he was a spy for the United States government. Certainly a fascinating fact, but hardly likely to alter Red Sox history.

But what if . . .

It was mid-August of 1939 and rookie Ted Williams was enjoying a superb first year in the majors. The cocky young hitter wasn't the least bit intimidated by big-league pitching, cruising along well above the .300 mark with 30 homers, while leading the league in RBIs with 95. The second-place Sox were playing a Sunday doubleheader with the league-leading New York Yankees at Fenway Park, and another large crowd was expected to come out and watch the young phenom from San Diego.

Berg. Moe Berg.

With war threatening in Europe, the United States and Britain held top-secret discussions about what to do if Germany attacked a neighboring nation. Intelligence suggested that Germany's plans were not limited to Poland or even Europe; Hitler was a madman and was willing to sacrifice untold German lives to gratify his own ego.

Hitler realized that the United States would hold the balance of power if Britain were drawn into the conflict, so Herr Hitler decided to make a preemptive diplomatic strike on the eve of his planned invasion of Poland. He contacted President Roosevelt and suggested a summit meeting. Roosevelt was completely taken aback by the offer, and he agreed only after hurried consultation with War Department officials and, secretly, representatives of British Prime Minister Neville Chamberlain.

Germany's bitter experience in the Great War made Hitler keenly aware that U.S. involvement on the side of the allies could tip the scale in any hostilities. His goal was clear. He wanted to convince the United States to side with them—or, at the very least, remain neutral in the event of a worldwide conflict. To that end, the führer would make an unprecedented visit to America to personally intervene with the president. While there, he would work his charismatic magic on the American populace.

With elaborate security measures in place, the two leaders agreed to meet at an undisclosed location in Cambridge, Massachusetts (actually on the campus of Harvard University). A full month of preparations followed, and the German leader arrived at a secluded Massachusetts airstrip on August 24, 1939. Hitler was encouraged and energized by the initial reception he received from U.S. government officials, and he looked forward to the next day's face-to-face meeting with the president. He was convinced in his own delusional mind that if Americans could see the bright future that his Aryan race would cultivate, they would eventually side with Germany. He would then be well on his way to having fulfilled his oft-stated dream: "Ven I goose-step down the strasse, I vant volks to look at me and say, 'There goes the greatest Hitler who ever lived!'"

The day before the crucial meeting was to be low-key for the Nazi leader, a day of reflection and preparation. Too much publicity could scuttle the talks before they began. Hitler wanted to use the day to relax and get a feel for what the average American was thinking. He wanted to soak up some of the uniquely American traditions, to establish a bond with the people, to become just plain "volks." His hosts had suggested weeks earlier that he take in a baseball game, that most American of pastimes. "If you wish to understand America, you'd better learn about baseball," the youthful, smiling attaché Jorg Brennerstein had admonished. Hitler was intrigued by the notion. If anyone knew the propaganda potential of sports it was he. Just three years earlier, in August of 1936, Germany had hosted the world at the Summer Olympics. He had used the event as an opportunity to portray Nazi Germany as a nation of tolerance and peace, and the scheme was largely successful. Plans were laid weeks in advance for the führer's foray to Fenway. Roosevelt would also be attending the doubleheader but would sit across the diamond from Hitler, behind the Red Sox dugout, for "security reasons."

The evening before the games, Hitler insisted on coming to the ballpark. Experience had taught him the value of knowing his stage before any big event. The tour guide, a representative of the Red Sox, had been instructed only to "give Herr Schicklgruber, an important visitor from overseas, a tour of Fenway Park." When Hitler saw the green left-field Wall, the small man with the Charlie Chaplin moustache smirked and said in German to his aides: "Only over my dead body will we have such an ugly wall in Berlin!" The guide then explained the fundamental rules of baseball and pointed out the foul poles down the first- and third-base lines. Again the führer scoffed, once more addressing his entourage in their native tongue. "As of September 1, all the Poles will be fair game." The guide thought them a very strange group.

Unbeknownst to Herr Hitler, his request to meet with Roosevelt had immediately unleashed a flurry of behind-the-scenes activity at all levels in Washington and other Western capitals. The seemingly casual and spontaneous ballpark suggestion had actually been part of a carefully orchestrated master plan, a bold and elaborate scheme engineered in cooperation with British and Canadian intelligence.

Moe Berg, the Red Sox catcher, was also an international spy. And he was a much better spy than he was a catcher. He had traveled to Japan in 1934 with an All-Star barnstorming team that included such legitimate All-Stars as Babe Ruth and Lou Gehrig. Berg, a .251 hitter, of whom it was accurately said, "He could speak a dozen languages and couldn't hit in any of them," was not there because of his baseball skills. His assignment was to gather intelligence on Japanese installations in the event of war. During his stay, Berg had learned of Japan's growing military might. The information that he obtained was passed up the line to the very highest levels of the U.S. government. Berg's skills as a spy were duly noted, and his stock rose accordingly. Of late he had also made trips to Germany—a kind of "catcher in the Rhineland"—and had been advising the U.S. government on Germany's readiness to create and deploy a nuclear bomb.

Early in 1939, President Roosevelt had decided that a bold move must be made: a declarative statement, a preemptive diplomatic strike that would emphatically announce America's adamant refusal to tolerate the likes of Hitler. But what should it be? The gesture must leave no doubt in anyone's mind about U.S. loyalties. It must achieve its ends definitively. The risks were immense, the implications far-reaching, but the alternative was unacceptable. American lives were at stake. Hitler was a madman, but a man of action; he would not be deterred by diplomacy or meaningless promises. They were just weapons in his arsenal of deception. The espionage reports submitted by Moe Berg and other government operatives had sent a chill down the backs of U.S. officials and their allies.

Hitler's overture to the United States was extremely presumptuous and blatantly transparent. Roosevelt was furious. How dare he assume that the world's greatest democracy would listen to the ravings of a power-mad tyrant? America would not sit idly by while its closest allies fought the fight for democracy. As for joining forces with this evil empire—that was unthinkable. Already Canada was sending men overseas, and some Americans were beginning to enlist in the Canadian armed forces.

Hitler's communication had come in the middle of crucial deliberations about an American response to events in Europe. U.S. ambassador to England Joseph P. Kennedy worked feverishly with British officialdom, including Winston Churchill, to come up with a plan. What at first was looked on with disbelief and disgust was now viewed as a godsend. Teams of trained military and diplomatic experts worked interminable hours on the plan. Never before had such a degree of cooperation existed among every level of government and among freedom-loving countries. The scheme was simple, but meticulously planned.

During the Red Sox's mid-August road trip to Washington to play the Senators—"First in war, first in peace, last in the American League"—much was going on behind the scenes. After an easy 7–2 series-opening victory, Ted Williams and Moe Berg slipped away from the visitor's clubhouse and were not seen again until a few hours before the next day's contest. Both men were evasive when teammates asked where they had been. Jimmie Foxx joked that they had probably been at a "****ing museum" and opined about the deleterious influence the intellectual Berg was having on the previously fun-loving rookie Williams.

Berg and Williams had actually been at the White House as guests of the president. Roosevelt had met with them and high-ranking War Department officials in the Oval Office. They began with small talk about baseball. Roosevelt and Berg seemed completely at ease, and Williams was his usual brash self. Three weeks later they were back in Boston for a four-game series with the New York Yankees. The first two games would be a double-header, the additional game added due to an early-season rainout.

Red Sox–Yankees games were always special, but this was to be a game like none other before or since. A single marksman would be stationed on the roof above the press box behind home plate. From his position, he would have a clear view of Hitler's seat, but little else. Therefore, it would be Berg's assignment to oversee the operation from field level. Hitler, along with assorted Reichstag officials, would be seated down the third-base line behind the Yankees dugout. From his position behind the plate, Berg would have the best view of the entire field and would be able to abort the mission should some unforeseen event take place. The catcher was now giving two sets of signals. Aside from his usual signs for the pitcher, he was also relaying signals to the man in the booth high above and behind him. After every half-inning he would enter the dugout and slip surreptitiously into the clubhouse, where he would report to an intermediary.

The danger was that innocent bystanders might also be killed or injured, and the War Department had brought in its top marksman to carry out the assassination. It was to happen with Ted Williams at bat. The prearranged signal for the sharpshooter to fire would be a tip of the hat from Williams. Berg would relay the sign from the Red Sox dugout, a position that allowed him a clear view across the diamond. With Williams at the plate, it was reasoned, patrons would be sure to be in their seats and focused on the man at home plate. Williams was to take the first pitch— something he almost always did in any case—step out of the batter's box, and touch the bill of his cap. That touch of the hat was the signal for the assassin to strike. The naturally effusive Williams had to be sure not to tip his hat at any other time or the consequences would be catastrophic.

"You're only young once, but you can be immature forever."

—Larry Andersen, pitcher

Berg and Williams would seem to be an unlikely pair to team up for anything. Berg was a back-up catcher: mature, well educated, well traveled, and couldn't hit a lick. Ted was a high school graduate, immature, headstrong, and already one of the best hitters in the league. Yet when the Red Sox management asked Berg to take the young ballplayer under his wing and instruct him in the intangibles of being a major league ballplayer, Moe and Ted formed an immediate bond. Williams admired Berg's reserve, his intelligence, his sophistication, and the air of mystery that surrounded him. He also took note of the way Berg handled himself around the press. For his part, Berg obviously admired the way that Williams hit, but there was something else too. He could see that Ted was a very intelligent, analytical man. Berg's education was obviously much more extensive, varied, and formal, but he admired Ted's enthusiasm for learning and his intellectual curiosity. This odd couple fed off each other's differences and shared that one overriding similarity.

Ted called Moe "Secret"; Moe, like everyone else, referred to Williams as the "Kid." The two could often be seen talking in hushed tones at the far end of the Red Sox clubhouse. Preoccupied by other matters, Williams was in the midst of a modest o-for-12 hitting slump.

Due to "security issues," Fenway patrons were not to be officially informed of Hitler's presence until just before game time. The real reason for the secrecy lay not in security concerns for Hitler but in safety concerns for the fans attending the game. However, word leaked out the previous day when Colonel Dave Egan overheard a conversation between two German officials in a Boston bar. His column in that day's *Boston American* was anything but understated: FÜHRER FUROR FORECAST FOR FENWAY, with the subhead "Williams in Hitting Funk." Government agents considered aborting the assassination attempt altogether. Only after prolonged pregame discussions did they decide that it would go ahead as scheduled. It was not unusual for politicians—even world leaders—to attend games as part of the Boston or American "experience." But this was not just any benign world leader. This was Herr Hitler. With the publicity he had been getting of late in newsreels and magazines—he had appeared on the cover of *Time* as their "Man of the Year" in 1938—no one could easily mistake Hitler for just another fan. His distinctive mustache and haughty, pompous demeanor would have made him stand out in any crowd. He took his seat, surrounded by members of his security and diplomatic team, behind the Yankees dugout.

The starting pitcher for the Red Sox in the opener was Lefty Grove, while Red Ruffing was slated to toe the rubber for the Yanks. If fans had been really attentive they would have noticed some small but, in retrospect, significant occurrences that day. For one thing, Berg, despite his .203 batting average, was tabbed to catch the game in place of the slightly more productive Johnny Peacock (.277). Before the game, Williams, at that stage of his career a very social ballplayer, avoided the media and other teammates and spoke only with Berg. Whenever Berg took his place behind home plate during warm-up, he glanced in the direction of the German delegation, stood, and then glanced furtively toward the press box, a small smile playing on his lips. It was such a minor thing that even if someone had noticed it, they would have had no reason to think it unusual. More noticeable was Berg's bizarre pitch-calling that day and the fact that Grove shook him off several times, on one occasion calling Moe to the mound and loudly berating him for his inattention to the game.

Berg, a New Jersey Jew, despised Hitler and everything he stood for. His reaction to the German leader was much more visceral and personal than his disdain for the regime in Japan.

He had confided that he felt uneasy at being in the bullpen "telling jokes" when he could be making a real contribution to the world. This was his chance to do just that.

President Roosevelt was slated to throw out the ceremonial first pitch in the opening contest. Hitler would be accorded the same honor in the second game. If all went well, there would be no second game; it would be postponed due to the untimely death of Adolf Hitler. Photographers had arranged through the Red Sox public relations staff for Ted Williams to be at the plate for both opening pitches to add drama and give an assist to next day's headline writers. To general applause, Roosevelt's wheelchair was maneuvered to a position halfway between the mound and home plate. From this location, the president was able to throw an almost perfect strike into Berg's glove. The appreciative crowd howled their delight as Williams swung wildly, intentionally missing the ball by two feet and almost falling to the ground with the feigned effort. The caption for this photo would offer numerous opportunities for punsters in the political and sporting press. Williams and Berg approached Roosevelt, shook his hand warmly, and presented him with the baseball.

After Roosevelt had been returned to his seat behind the Red Sox dugout, the umpire yelled, "Play ball!" and the game was under way. Grove struck out the side in the top of the first to the delight of the highly partisan crowd. Leading off for the Red Sox in the bottom half of the inning, Joe Cronin singled to right field. Next up was Bobby Doerr, who forced the count to 3–1 and then walked. Jimmie Foxx was up next and walked on just four pitches, loading the bases. Ted came to the plate with the roar of 33,000 adoring fans ringing in his ears. Looking toward the Yankees dugout, he saw that many fans were still filing in, obscuring his view of the German dictator. Not a good time, he decided. Turning his attention to the pitcher, he drove the second pitch high into the right-field bleachers, some 470 feet from home plate.

Williams rounded the bases and crossed the plate with his head down, without acknowledging his waiting teammates or tipping his cap despite the joyous, entreating cries from the crowd.

Ted's second time at bat came in the fourth frame. This time Berg saw autograph seekers obscuring his view of Hitler and gave Ted the signal to abort. Ignoring the constant chatter of Yankees catcher Bill Dickey, the Kid lined a double to right field. The score remained 4–0 when he came to the plate, again with the bases loaded, in the seventh inning. Ted went over the plan in his mind. He was nervous but determined. The first pitch came in from Ruffing, a fat fastball that Ted watched go by. The umpire yelled, "Strike one!" and Ted remained in the batter's box.

Despite the fact that it was Williams' first year, word of his hitting habits had spread throughout the American League. Ruffing knew that this was when Williams was most dangerous. He had seen his fastball and would adjust his bat speed accordingly. But Ruffing was a clever pitcher. He also knew Ted's growing reputation as one of the most selective and patient hitters in baseball. He had deliberately not thrown his best fastball because he knew that Williams would be taking all the way. Williams got the thumbs up from Berg, and double-checked the führer's position. Just as he was about to step out and tip his cap, a beer vendor walked directly in front of Hitler. The Nazi was having a Narragansett! Ted was beside himself with frustration and anger.

My next pitch will catch the rookie napping, the veteran pitcher thought. Staring in for the catcher's signal, Ruffing went into his windup and released the ball. The ball came in hard and high but well within the strike zone. Acting upon instinct, Ted swung at the pitch and drove the ball on a low trajectory to right field. At first it looked as if it would be caught by the right fielder, but the ball continued to rise as it passed over his head to land deep in the bleachers. It had exited the field so quickly that it landed almost before the cry went up from the assembled throng. Williams ran the bases

The führer, sitting in the stands at Fenway, reacts to a bonehead play at third base during game one of the doubleheader.

quickly, head down, and appeared angry with himself. As he was passing third base on the last leg of his journey home, he glanced toward the Yankees dugout and then toward the press box. With fists clenched, he issued a string of profanities as he crossed home plate. They were lost in the din of celebration.

He thought of suddenly and deliberately lifting the hat from his head and acknowledging the cheers from the crowd. But the crowd was now standing and cheering wildly. It would be much too dangerous for the innocent bystanders. Ted had reacted on a hitter's instinct, and it had proven disastrous. Williams again crossed the plate without shaking hands with his teammates or tipping his hat, and he disappeared into the dugout.

Williams came to the plate again in the bottom of the eighth, with a man on first and the Sox lead now at 8–0. As instructed, Ted looked at the seats behind the Yankees dugout and stared at the place where Hitler was supposed to be. To his chagrin, he was not there! Ted caught a glimpse of him as he went down the runway with a bodyguard, heading for the washroom. *He's the only one in this ballpark who would leave when I come to the plate!* thought an exasperated Ted. *Damn that Narragansett!* He looked toward the press box and bent down to pick up a handful of dirt, the signal to abort. The assassination would have to happen in the second game.

On the second delivery, almost as an afterthought, Ted swung and hit a screaming line drive that exited the playing field no more than three feet above the fence and just inches to the fair side of the right-field foul pole. The large Fenway crowd was delirious, savoring their team's command of the hated rivals from New York. Again Ted did not tip his cap as he crossed home plate, and this time a small chorus of boos could be heard from behind the Red Sox dugout.

The game ended in a 10–0 Red Sox shutout, with Williams driving in all 10 Red Sox runs. Fans went to get drinks and hot dogs before settling in for the second game, featuring the Yankees' Lefty Gomez against the Red Sox's Eldon Auker. Berg and Ted huddled between games, ignoring the media, fans, and fellow players. Their conversation appeared animated, even heated at times.

The second game got under way, and Hitler was now officially announced to the capacity crowd. A wave of jeers and catcalls, sprinkled with a smattering of dutifully polite applause, greeted the announcement and continued during his escorted trip to the pitching mound. A group of about one hundred bleacherites stood and held their arms straight out, with middle fingers extended. Soon the entire ballpark followed suit, with each section rising in turn in a wave of extended arms and fingers. Hitler saw this, misunderstood the intent, and smiling broadly, returned a crisp Heil Hitler salute. Thus the "wave" was born.

Despite the now oppressive heat, the Nazi leader was wearing his uniform. He presented a ridiculous figure to the festive, shirtsleeved Fenway crowd. Moe Berg settled behind the plate for the time-honored first pitch ceremony, and Ted Williams again stood in the batter's box for the sake of the hoard of photographers and newsreel people crowded around the infield. Berg was dreading the traditional handshake that followed such ceremonies, and he considered snubbing the leader or even spitting in his face, but he realized that this gesture, although personally satisfying, would destroy the plan. Despite his stellar offensive performance in game one of the twin bill, Williams was still seething from the mission's failure.

What if the same thing happened in game two? *I can't let that happen*, he decided with finality.

Hitler had never been a great athlete, but, not wanting to look foolish, he had practiced throwing baseballs on a vacant Harvard soccer field with the pleasant young American attaché assigned to him. He would throw the ceremonial first pitch, shake hands with Berg and Williams, and return to his seat to general applause. The gesture would prove that he was one of them, "der kleine Mann," just your average Adolf, thought der führer.

Hitler took the baseball from the Fenway Park official and rested his right foot on the rubber as he had been coached to do. He went into his version of a pitching windup—right arm extended as if in a bizarre Heil Hitler salute, left leg raised as if in a modified goose-step—and released the ball. It went slowly but amazingly straight and true toward Berg's waiting glove. As it crossed the middle of the plate, Ted Williams' bat suddenly whipped around at lightning speed. The crack of bat on ball was like a gunshot, and the ball rocketed off the Louisville Slugger with the speed of an assassin's bullet, striking the dictator squarely between the eyes. The Hun was stunned. He staggered backward slightly, righted himself momentarily, then pitched face first to the ground, as if poleaxed. He was dead before he hit the mound.

Chaos reigned. The Red Sox trainer rushed onto the field to render assistance. With help from the clubhouse boy, he turned the lifeless body over. Eyewitnesses later reported that the stitches of the ball had left an angry red mark resembling a swastika on the führer's forehead. Under it, the barely visible words "William Harridge, American League President" were imbedded backward between his still-wide-open eyes. Berg and Williams were hustled off the field as quickly as possible, and both dugouts were ringed with Boston police officers. After a brief, inappropriate burst of upbeat organ music ("The

And that's how Ted Williams' bat saved the free world.

Hallelujah Chorus"), and a slight squawk of reverb from the ancient Fenway speakers, the public address announcer asked people to remain calm and file out of the stadium in an orderly fashion.

FÜHRER FELLED AT FENWAY screamed the headline in the next day's *Boston Traveling American Globe*, above the subhead "Williams' Deadly Stroke Returns." NUMBER NINE NAILS NAZI announced the *Boston Postal Global American*, over the sub "Ted a True Dead Pull Hitter." The *Boston Global American Traveler* proclaimed HITTER HEILS HITLER, with the subhead "Williams Back to Form." The *Boston Bugle* trumpeted TEDDY SOURS KRAUT with the subhead "Perfect Day for Williams." The *Christian Silent Monitor* suggested KID 1, KRAUT 0. SPLINTER CORKS SPHINCTER announced the underground *Boston Basement*, with the sub "Ted Swings at First Pitch." The *Boston American Traveling Globe* put matters in pragmatic perspective with TEDDY ON A TEAR, subhead "Hitler Dead; Sox Alive." The *Boston Patriot* said simply: WILL AMERICA LET NAZIS FLOURISH? NUMBER NINE TO SWINE FROM RHINE: "NEIN!" Only the hard-to-please Colonel Egan decided to take a slightly different tack in his column entitled WILLIAMS FAILS TO TIP HAT TO CROWD, with the subhead "Killing Hitler Just Not Enough." The foreign press was more impressed. The *London Times* proclaimed the lethal line drive "the line shot heard round the world."

Ted explained to reporters that he found it "tough to lay off a pitch in the strike zone."

The seat in which Hitler had been sitting was subsequently painted red, white, and blue and remains there to this very day as a symbol of Freedom's victory over Tyranny. The baseball that had killed Hitler went directly to the newly created Hall of Fame in Cooperstown, New York. From that day forward, a line drive up the middle was known in baseball parlance as a "hun stunner." The Nazi's autopsy declared that the cause of death was "accidental death by line drive."

> "Every time I look at a Yankees hat I see a swastika tilted just a little off kilter."
> —Chairman Lee

■ ■ ■

The death of Hitler proved to be the third strike for the Third Reich. With Hitler dead, rival factions within the Nazi Party battled for control of the government. One faction saw the hope of world domination as sheer folly; the other continued to follow the teachings of Hitler and his *Mein Kampf*. The air of invincibility and solidarity that once cloaked the Party dissolved into bickering and outright dissension. The German people began to see them for what they were, and support dwindled. Grassroots pockets of opposition began to form. At first they were brutally crushed, but each successive movement fueled further dissent, and the brutality of the ruling party spawned further disenchantment with the government.

Eventually, elections would be held and a more moderate coalition government formed. Europe and the rest of the world breathed a bit easier. Japan was now isolated and retreated within its island fortress.

■ ■ ■

Meanwhile, baseball in the United States continued to thrive. Ted Williams and Moe Berg watched world tensions ease with a degree of personal satisfaction, although they were unable to share the true details with teammates or fans until decades later. Soon the Red Sox were much more concerned with immediate problems at home. Their enemies were once again the Yankees and other AL foes. For the 1939 season, rookie Williams batted .327 with 39 homers and, although there was not yet an official Rookie of the Year award, no less an authority than Babe Ruth gave him the unofficial designation. *Total Baseball* records that he was the last major league rookie to hit over .300 and kill a world leader in the same season. In Ted's sophomore campaign, he sagged slightly with 23 homers and 113 ribbies, but he raised his average to .344. In 1941, Ted did it all, batting .406 to become the first player in more than a decade to hit the elite mark.

In 1942 the Red Sox recorded their highest winning percentage since the glory days of 1915, as Ted captured his first Triple Crown on the strength of 36 homers, 137 RBIs, and a .356 batting average. (The batting average actually constituted a 50-point "slump" from his 1941 average.)

In 1943, expectations were running high throughout New England. The Red Sox had finished second to the Yankees four out of five years from 1938 to 1942. Could they finally beat the Bronx Bombers? The answer is yes. With Williams at the peak of his hitting powers and a stellar supporting cast that included Bobby Doerr, Johnny Pesky, and Dom DiMaggio, they captured the American League pennant by eight games, out-dueling the New York juggernaut captained by the Yankee Clipper Joe DiMaggio. Ted tore the cover off the ball in 1943, hitting .396 with 48 homers and an incredible 155 RBIs. His average was at .396 going into the final two games of the season, when he was walked eight consecutive times.

Ted was named MVP in 1943 and again in 1944, when he recorded his second .400 season in three years. He added 45 homers and 159 RBIs en route to the second Triple Crown of his young career. More important, the Red Sox won another pennant and went on to defeat the St. Louis Cardinals in four games in the World Series.

In 1945, the Sox hit full stride early in the season and the word *dynasty* was being bandied about freely in the Boston press. The Sox finished with a record of 100–54, seven-and-a-half games ahead of the second-place Yankees. Ted Williams was in his sixth year in the majors and was now a seasoned veteran. He started the season batting .455 at the end of May, and although he slumped somewhat in the heat of August, he maintained the .400 level into September. His final mark of .404 represented the third time in five years that he had reached the elusive mark. The World Series of 1945 pitted the Red Sox against the Chicago Cubs. The Red Sox won the Series in seven games, the final game a nail-biter decided on a tenth-inning home run by Ted Williams in Wrigley Field. It was the only opposing home run ball in franchise history not thrown back onto the field by Cubs fans. "Are you ****ing nuts?" said the fan who caught the ball when asked why he didn't throw it back. "This was Ted ****ing Williams."

■ ■ ■

Williams became the darling of all New England, and despite occasional fits of temper and ill-advised remarks to the sporting press, fans thronged to Fenway Park to watch him and his teammates perform. With several newspapers vying for the consumer dollar, attempts were made to sensationalize Williams' every mistake—on and off the field—but these transparent efforts were met with hostility from the fans. Some even went so far as to boycott the newspaper of Colonel Egan, who had been especially vicious in his commentary. Egan left the newspaper business and later sold vacuum cleaners door to door. His slogan was consistent with his negative approach to life: "These vacuums really suck!"

The rivalry with the New York Yankees grew even more intense as the two teams dominated the American League standings into the early fifties. When the Bosox failed to win the pennant, the Yankees usually did, and baseball prospered in the densely populated northeastern United States as a result. Baseball also continued to flourish in Japan and, ironically, began to blossom in Germany as well. German tourists, coming to Fenway to view the historic site of Hitler's assassination, returned home with stories of "die Boston Rot Socken." Eventually Japanese and German ballplayers would play alongside North American and Latin American ballplayers, and the major leagues would become a genuine league of nations.

Ted finished his career in 1961, deciding to play an extra year when his home-run totals stood at 701 at the end of the 1960 campaign. He ended his career with an even 730, a record that would stand until Hank Aaron finally surpassed it in 1974.

Throughout the remainder of his Hall of Fame career, Ted Williams would continue to tip his cap whenever he crossed the plate after a home run. When the occasional leather-lunged fan with too much to drink booed him lustily after an error or strikeout, Ted tipped his cap especially high, with a sly, enig-matic smile on his face. And he always—always—tipped his cap to sportswriters. Only he, Moe Berg, and the United States gov-ernment appreciated the true significance of the gesture. Ted was never again asked to pose at the plate when world leaders—or even U.S. Democrats—threw out the first pitch.

After he retired, Ted could never walk down the street with-out someone commenting: "There goes the greatest hitter who ever lived! There goes the man who went three for three in a doubleheader, four for four if you count killing Hitler."

Chapter 5
Fenway's Other Wall

*"The time is always right to
do what is right."*
—Martin Luther King Jr.

*"They say I was born too soon. I say the
doors were opened too late."*
—James "Cool Papa" Bell, legendary player with
the Homestead Grays of the Negro Leagues

When Bostonians talk about the "Wall," they are usually referring to the 37-foot green barricade that has played such a significant role in Red Sox history. The left-field Wall has become as much a part of Red Sox folklore as the baseball immortals who played in its shadow. It is as much a symbol of Boston as the Great Wall is of China. But there was once another wall at Fenway Park, and it was much more daunting and impregnable than even the Green Monster. This "white wall" is just as much a part of Red Sox history as the one beneath which Ted and Yaz and Jim Ed once patrolled. Invisible but all too real, it was the barrier that kept blacks out of the Red Sox major league organization until 1959. But like all walls, this wall of intolerance had two sides: it can be argued that for at least a decade it also kept the Red Sox out of contention for postseason

> I've seen it happen so often. A white guy with little natural ability shows some false hustle and becomes the manager's pet. Meanwhile, a gifted black athlete gets the job done with seeming ease and he's considered a loafer, gets a bad reputation, and ends up in the manager's doghouse. Most managers are guys who scrambled and hustled to stay in the majors—guys like Billy Martin and Don Zimmer. They resent anyone to whom it comes easy. They prefer the scrappy little guys with few skills, because they look at them and see themselves.

glory. It has often been said of the Green Monster that "it giveth and it taketh away." The white wall of Fenway gave us nothing and took away so very much. And in so doing, it influenced the fate of the Red Sox in a much more profound way than the infamous left-field structure ever did.

On April 16, 1945, three black ballplayers from the Negro Leagues—second baseman Marvin Williams, outfielder Sam Jethroe (who in 1950 would be named NL Rookie of the Year for the crosstown Boston Braves), and shortstop Jackie Robinson—took the field at Fenway Park. It was the eve of Opening Day and they were there thanks to the persistence of a Jewish Boston city councilman named Isadore Muchnick. The Red Sox had been virtually blackmailed, or at least shamed, into giving them a tryout. After general manager Eddie Collins' disingenuous assertion that "we have never had a single request for a tryout by a colored applicant," they had to be there. These black ballplayers served a necessary role. They were there to show the press that the Red Sox were an open-minded, progressive organization dedicated only to fielding the best team possible.

In the midst of their tryout, however, an anonymous cry came from the smattering of team personnel gathered behind the dugout to watch: "Get that nigger off the field!"

It is uncertain to this day who uttered the remark that rang out so clearly on that beautiful spring afternoon. But that one racist sentence denied countless qualified black players a chance to play for the Boston Red Sox. It also denied the Red Sox a chance to win several world championships. In fact, it could be argued that there are actually two curses on the Red Sox: the much bally-hooed curse of the Bambino and the less talked about but equally devastating curse of Jackie Robinson. One curse was born of reckless action by Red Sox ownership, the other of negligent and shortsighted inaction by Red Sox ownership.

The Red Sox always get these red-haired guys like John Kennedy and Jack Brohamer and Frank Duffy. They always have to have red hair and freckles so that the guys from Southie will come to the ballgames. It's always been that way. My theory is that they got Lynn McGlothen for that reason. They didn't know that he was black until he arrived. They drafted him and with that name they must have thought he was from friggin' Scotland, not Louisiana.

When the tryout was over, the three black players were told they had done well and were asked to fill in application forms. "You'll be hearing from us," they were assured by coach Hugh Duffy. Later that day Marvin Williams expressed the skepticism that they all shared. "We'll hear from the Red Sox like we'll hear from Adolf Hitler," he said. Robinson and the other black players were not signed by the Boston Red Sox that day or any other day. In fact, the Sox did not bring up a black ballplayer until 14 years later, when Pumpsie Green—who was no Jackie Robinson—arrived in Boston in 1959. Boston's American League flagship team holds the unenviable distinction of being the last franchise in all of baseball to integrate its lineup. They had the opportunity to be first; instead they were dead last.

> I would have batted Jackie Robinson after Williams in the lineup. That way you would have had the snail people early in the lineup banging the ball, and the bottom half of the lineup would be a running lineup. It would have been amazing! And then when Dominic DiMaggio retired, they would bring in the little black kid from Birmingham, Willie Mays, because the doors would then be open, and the Red Sox would have been seen as an oasis of racial tolerance. Branch Rickey, the Dodgers' president, was a staunch Protestant, and he did it with Brooklyn.

Jackie Robinson subsequently entered the Brooklyn Dodgers organization, played minor league ball in Montreal, and came up to the parent team on April 15, 1947, to become the first African American to play in the major leagues. Dodgers president Branch Rickey took some initial criticism for the move, but he will go down in American history, along with Jackie himself, as a pioneer—the men who integrated baseball. As courageous and laudable as Rickey's move was, it was not done entirely out of altruism or idealism. It was based in pragmatism and baseball savvy. Rickey knew that Robinson could play. He also knew that Robinson's exciting brand of baseball would sell tickets and improve his team. He was right. During his time in Brooklyn, Jackie was a spark plug who led his team to six pennants and, finally, a World Series victory in 1955. He finished his 10-year career with a .311 batting average, 137 homers, and 197 stolen bases.

More important than the relatively modest raw statistics were the intangibles that Robinson brought to the often staid and conservative old game of baseball. With his frantic activity on the base paths, he disrupted the concentration and rhythm of pitchers throughout the National League, leading to countless scoring opportunities for the Dodgers. Jackie stole home 19 times, 5 times in a single season! There is no statistic for desire, but if there were, he would be among the all-time leaders. In 1949, Jackie captured the MVP award on the strength of a league-leading .342 batting average, 16 homers, and 124 RBIs. He also topped the senior circuit in stolen bases with 37 and carried the Dodgers past the St. Louis Cardinals by a single game to capture the NL pennant. He was an impact player before the term existed. He made things happen. Above all else, Jackie Robinson was a winner.

The thing about Robinson is that he could play anywhere. If the Red Sox had signed him, they would probably have initially made him a utility player. A super sub. And he was such a scrappy guy that he would have done well at first base, he would have played second when Doerr needed a rest, he'd have played short when Pesky needed a rest, and he would have almost definitely played the hot corner. And he would have played in the outfield when he needed to. Just think of the statues they would have built to him. Jackie and Ted, black and white, side by side, outside Fenway.

■ ■ ■

In the late forties, Birmingham, Alabama, was home to the Red Sox Double-A farm team. They played their home games at Rickwood Field, also home to the Negro Leagues' Birmingham Black Barons. The Red Sox organization thus was afforded easy, almost exclusive access to any and all Baron players with major league potential. In 1948, a young 17-year-old sensation named Willie Mays was playing for the Barons. The Red Sox knew all about him. They could have signed him on the spot. They didn't. Years later, Mays told Ted Williams, a hitter whom he idolized, "I always thought I was supposed to play with you in Boston." For his part, Williams gave Mays his highest accolade: "If DiMaggio wasn't the

A Red Sox scout recommended signing Willie Mays from the Birmingham, Alabama, Black Barons. And they could have done so for next to nothing, but the Red Sox declined and one of the greatest players in baseball history went to the New York Giants. To think Jackie Robinson, Ted Williams, and Willie Mays could have played together on the same Red Sox teams of the early fifties: Jackie, the Kid, and the Say Hey Kid. It boggles the mind.

"There have been only two geniuses in the world: Willie Mays and Willie Shakespeare."
—Tallulah Bankhead, actress

greatest all-around player I ever saw, then Mays probably was." An outfield of Williams, Mays, and Dom DiMaggio—and later, Williams, Mays, and Jackie Jensen—was within their reach. But, like Robinson, Willie Mays was black.

Thus, in a period of five years, the Red Sox lost two of the greatest players in baseball history. They also lost the respect of countless future black stars who looked to New York's Dodgers and Giants, and not to Boston, as oases of tolerance. Some feel that today's self-absorbed major league stars have no sense of history. As recently as the end of the 20th century, however, black players were vocal about not playing in Boston. Some even went so far as to have "no-trade-to-Boston" clauses in their contracts because of this perceived history of racism. It may well have been Mo Vaughn, proudly bearing Robinson's No. 42 on his uniform, who turned the tide in baseball circles.

What can you say about a team that would pass on a chance to sign Jackie Robinson and Willie Mays? Well, you can say they were stupid. Or you can say they were very, very stupid. Or you can say they were very, very stupid . . . and racist. How stupid and racist were they? So stupid that, apparently, they were waiting for a player of Pumpsie Green's caliber to arrive. Robinson

"The Red Sox had the habit of always bringing in black and Latino players who were on their last legs. They brought Aparicio in when he was at the end of his career. Same with Marichal and Perez and Harper."

—Chairman Lee

In Howard Bryant's important book *Shut Out*, the author reveals that after Green's arrival in Boston, Jackie Robinson, then three years into retirement, "called to remind Green that the two were, in a way, bookends to the long story of baseball integration." According to Bryant, Robinson went on to tell Green that "his achievement was by no means anticlimactic, but equally historic, for the last team to integrate likely suffered from an ingrained, deeply entrenched form of racism that was possibly worse than anything Robinson himself had ever endured."

and Mays are now in the Hall of Fame and have become icons of American culture. Pumpsie Green's main function with the Red Sox was playing sideline catch with the very welcoming Ted Williams. Sadly, and through no fault of Green's, his main legacy is as a symbol of the fact that the Red Sox were the last baseball team to integrate. He is the flip side of Jackie Robinson. Robinson symbolizes first; Green symbolizes last. No one pays much attention to the last man to conquer Everest, or the last person to use the telephone. If the people who brought Robinson to baseball are heroes of American baseball, those who kept him from Fenway Park are necessarily the villains.

Ironically, baseball aside, Boston has a good—even enviable—record in America's history of sports integration. The Boston Celtics were the first major sports franchise in the post-Depression era to hire a black coach. They were also the first to draft a black player. Even the Boston Bruins, playing in a sport where the puck is usually the only black thing on the ice, featured the first black

Pumpsie Green's Major League Stats (1959–63)

- **1959:** 50 G/1 HR/.233 AVG
- **1960:** 133 G/3 HR/.242 AVG
- **1961:** 88 G/6 HR/.260 AVG
- **1962:** 56 G/2 HR/.231 AVG
- **1963:** (with New York Mets): 17 G/1 HR/.278 AVG

Notes:

- Pumpsie's career ran five years, in which time he had 13 home runs, a .246 batting average, and 12 stolen bases. He was caught stealing 10 times.
- Hall of Famer Jackie Robinson played 10 seasons, batting a career .311 with 137 home runs and 197 stolen bases. He was caught stealing just 30 times.
- Hall of Famer Willie Mays played 22 seasons, hit 660 home runs, and batted .302 over his career. He stole 338 bases.

"Subconsciously the Red Sox wanted Pumpsie to fail, to justify the fact that they were the last major league team to integrate."

—Chairman Lee

player in NHL history. That was in 1958, the year before Green took the field in a Red Sox uniform.

During that same baseball era, when Jackie Robinson and Willie Mays and Hank Aaron and Monte Irvin were changing the very nature of the game—the period many consider to be baseball's golden era—the Boston Red Sox were mired in the dark ages. They were perennial bridesmaids, coming close in '46, '48, and '49 but never quite able to seal the deal. In 1947, Robinson's rookie year with the Dodgers, the Sox finished third in the AL; the next year they finished second, then second again, then third, then third again. Then they started to drop, finishing sixth in 1952 and fourth the next four seasons. In two of those seasons, the Red Sox fell short of the pennant by a single game; another time it was by a slim four-game margin.

During these years, the Sox had offensive weapons that were beyond dispute. Ted Williams was undoubtedly the best hitter in the game. Dom DiMaggio was a great fielder and a superb hitter, and he and Johnny Pesky were unsurpassed in their ability to get on base for Ted to drive home. Bobby Doerr was a superb hitter as well and a defensive gem at second. Southpaw Mel Parnell, whose career years were identical to Robinson's, anchored a pitching staff that also boasted right-handed starter/reliever Ellis Kinder and brilliant young Mickey McDermott. In short, they had great hitters, solid pitching, and ownership with deep pockets. But they still lacked something.

Books have been written trying to identify that something, that intangible that kept them from finally beating out the hated Yankees. They certainly lacked speed and aggressiveness on the base paths. They featured a station-to-station offense, except when the Ted Williams Express cleared the tracks with another home run. But there was more to it than that. The knock on Tom Yawkey's Red Sox was that they were pampered and coddled ballplayers, idolized by their millionaire owner but seldom challenged to think or act as a team, in the truest sense of that word. Ted Williams was universally admired for his abilities, his desire, and his work ethic, but he was too tied up in his personal quest for perfection to rally the team. They needed a leader, not a figurehead, not a clubhouse speechmaker, but a genuine on-field general who would lead by example. There were none in sight.

■ ■ ■

If Ted and Jackie had played together, would they have gotten along? They were both fiery, temperamental individuals. In a letter to *Times-Picayune* columnist Bill Keefe, Jackie once drew the following comparison: "I'll admit I have not been subservient, but would you use the same adjective to describe a white ballplayer—say Ted Williams, who is, more often than I, involved in controversial matters?" Indeed, Ted had a record of spitting at fans and making obscene gestures in response to boos and catcalls. Jackie had to endure much worse treatment and couldn't permit himself any reaction.

Proof, in Black and White

In 1972, my third major league season, I met Scott Russell, a mild-mannered superstar of baseball statistics way before Bill James. He was also one of the foremost tutors of a fledgling writer named Peter Gammons. Russell's research clearly shows the immediate and practical impact of blacks on the game of baseball:

> Any attempt to prove how black players would have fared in the so-called major leagues before 1947 would be pure conjecture. Nevertheless, we certainly can prove beyond a doubt a sustained statistical superiority once these players were given the opportunity to compete with their white counterparts. For the purposes of this analysis, only players that were rookies in the NL beyond 1947 and in the AL beyond 1948 will be considered, because that was the beginning of "equal opportunity." Regardless of what records white players had set before Jackie Robinson, black players have now surpassed practically all. Such records as Joe DiMaggio's 56-consecutive-game hit streak could not possibly have been set while batting against black and Hispanic fielders.
>
> In the modern era, Mark McGwire set a home-run record that "could never be broken." Tell that to Barry Bonds. Stolen bases? New standards have been set and records shattered by black ballplayers. Consider Maury Wills stealing an unheard-of 104 bases—only to be surpassed by Lou Brock, Rickey Henderson, and Vince Coleman. Babe Ruth's mark of 714 homers was supposedly unassailable. Meet Henry Aaron. In a period of less than 30 years

(continued on next page)

after Robinson, blacks have destroyed many of the significant records previously thought to be unbreakable and sacrosanct.

The National League cornered the market on the great black and Latino players in the fifties and especially in the sixties, which I consider the golden age. Keep in mind that during the sixties the incredible Roberto Clemente could not even start for the NL All-Stars because of the presence of three guys named Willie Mays, Henry Aaron, and Frank Robinson. So dominant were the NL All-Stars that the NL went 16–2 in All-Star Games from 1960 to 1975!

The AL was so shamefully slow to recruit these great black athletes that Frank Robinson, in the twilight of his Hall of Fame career, was traded to the Baltimore Orioles in 1966 and immediately won the Triple Crown! The AL did not develop a great slugger of its own until the arrival of Reggie Jackson in Oakland!

The entrance of Jackie Robinson into the major leagues in 1947 did not herald the beginning of a flood of great Negro League players, but rather a slow trickle. Many great players—in actual fact many greater even than Robinson—still languished in the Negro Leagues because of the prejudice, fear, and apathy of owners. Many of these all-time greats were never given the opportunity to show America what they could accomplish. But oh, the few that were given that chance! Pioneers such as Robinson in the NL and Larry Doby, the first black to play in the AL, made a tremendous impact on the game. Considering the impact of these few players, one can only imagine

(continued on next page)

what might have been. Names such as Josh Gibson, Oscar Charleston, Leroy "Satchel" Paige, Judy Johnson, Roy Williams, Ray Dandridge, Jud Wilson, James "Cool Papa" Bell, Buck Leonard, Pop Lloyd, Buck O'Neil, Roy Partlow, Willie Wells, Dick Lundy, Newt Allen, Martin Dihigo, Smokey Joe Williams, Jimmie Crutchfield, Leon Day, Ted "Double Duty" Radcliffe, Ted Page, Piper Davis, Mule Settles, and Luis Tiant Sr. should be as well known as those of Willie Mays and Hank Aaron and Ted Williams and Mickey Mantle and Dizzy Dean. The fact that they are not illustrates a shameful chapter in American history.

Recently, at a sports memorabilia show in East Boston, I had the thrill of meeting Maury Wills, the great Dodgers shortstop and legendary base stealer. Upon congratulating the diminutive Mr. Wills on his great career, I mentioned the remarkable job he had done with current L.A. Dodgers leadoff man and offensive catalyst Dave Roberts. Roberts, a career minor leaguer until his path crossed with Wills, was tutored in the fine art of taking a lead, studying a pitcher's tendencies, getting the proper jump, and how to bunt. I frankly suggested that Wills' former teammate, the speedy Willie Davis, possessed far greater speed than Wills.

"Exactly," replied Wills. "If speed were the only requirement of base stealing, Willie Davis would've stolen twice as many as I did." So, the speed that the great black and Hispanic athletes brought to the game had to be augmented with technique, prowess, and mental skills well beyond mere athleticism.

(continued on next page)

At the same show, I met the great Monte Irvin, Hall of Famer, Negro League great, and former special assistant to the commissioner of baseball. Mr. Irvin was inducted into the Hall in 1973 after starring with the miraculous New York Giants of 1951; in fact, he led the NL in RBIs that year and hit a torrid .394 in the World Series! I had done a great deal of reading about the history of the Negro Leagues, and Mr. Irvin could not possibly have been more gracious in sharing his thoughts with me.

"Mr. Irvin," I asked, "I realize that you played alongside the great Willie Mays, considered by many to be the greatest ballplayer of all time, but I've heard so much about Oscar Charleston. Tell me, was Oscar Charleston the equal of Willie Mays?" Irvin pondered the question for a few moments and then responded thoughtfully.

"No, Oscar Charleston was not the equal of Willie Mays. . . . He was better than Willie Mays."

I was taken aback. "Mr. Irvin," I replied, "it is hard to believe that God could've created a better ballplayer than Willie Mays." He went on to explain that Mays was a better outfielder but that Charleston was a superior hitter who "if he had been allowed to play in the major leagues, would have batted over .400 for at least six seasons.

"I suggest that the vast majority of Americans— even fanatic baseball fans—have never heard the name, let alone know anything of his accomplishments." Monte Irvin concluded by saying, "It's a shame that people were denied the opportunity to see him play."

Shame, that's the very word I would use to describe it.

Remarkably, Williams' and Robinson's paths had crossed years earlier. In 1936, Jackie, the star of Muir Tech, and Ted, the star of Hoover High School, both earned places on the Pomona, California, tournament all-star squad. When the two men met and talked years later, Jackie was impressed, calling Ted "a fine person." For his part, when he was inducted into baseball's Hall of Fame in Cooperstown in 1966, Ted Williams made an eloquent plea for the induction of more Negro League players into the Hall, players, he said, "who are not here only because they were not given the chance." He then added, "Baseball gives every American boy a chance to excel. Not just to be as good as someone else, but to be better. This is the nature of man and the name of the game." At another time he admitted, "I'm thankful that I was given the chance to play baseball. . . . I've thought many a time, what would have happened to me if I hadn't had a chance. A chill goes up my back when I think I might have been denied this if I had been black." Ted Williams was ready. Why weren't the Red Sox?

But what if . . .

In late autumn of 1944 Tom Yawkey was walking through the pines on his massive 50,000-acre South Carolina estate. His wife was spending the weekend back in Boston, and Yawkey had the entire seaside property to himself, save for a handful of resident staff members. He carried a shotgun in the event that he encountered any of the plentiful game birds that inhabited the retreat, but on this beautiful fall day the weapon was little more than a prop, an excuse to enjoy the serenity and the solitude. As he ambled down the well-worn trail near the ocean, he was daydreaming about the prospects for his Red Sox when the war came to an end. Ted would be back of course, and so would most of the other regulars. *There's still something missing on that team, goddamn it*, he thought to himself as he followed the path that bordered a small salt marsh.

Preoccupied with his thoughts, he slipped on a moss-covered rock and fell backward. As he reached out his right arm to restore his balance, he felt a sharp stab of pain just above his wrist. A cottonmouth water moccasin slithered away, having delivered its venom. The olive-colored reptile was at least three-and-a-half feet long. Yawkey immediately recognized the coloration and the distinctive body crossbands with their borders extending around and across the yellowish underbelly. There was no doubt that this was the pit viper that local residents feared so much. Two years earlier an elderly man on a neighboring farm had been bitten by the same species of snake and had died a painful death. Panic rose in Yawkey as he turned to trudge the half mile back to his mansion.

When he finally reached the courtyard, his caretaker—a black man named Joe Armstrong—saw him and quickly realized that something was wrong. He rushed to his employer's side and half supported, half carried him indoors, settling him on the couch. Armstrong called the doctor's office. The office was closed for the weekend and when he tried to call the physician at home, there was no answer. After repeated attempts, the doctor's wife finally answered, only to say that her husband was attending an expectant mother and would be at least three hours getting to the estate.

The caretaker, a native of South Carolina, knew about cottonmouths; while their bite is seldom fatal, it can be excruciatingly painful. Realizing that excessive movement would only intensify the effect of the poison, Armstrong asked Yawkey to remain as still as possible. He examined the bite and noted that the redness and swelling had already begun. A large blister began to form, along with a discolored bruise. The Red Sox owner was nauseated and vomiting. He fainted several times and had to be revived. While he lapsed in and out of consciousness he started to hallucinate. The servant, trying to take his own mind off the distressing tableau and at the same time comfort his patient, began to address Yawkey in a soothing, almost singsong tone.

The two men had little in common save for a love of baseball. Joe, a former batboy for the Birmingham Black Barons, started talking about the other side of baseball, which he knew so well. He talked about Josh Gibson and Satchel Paige and Buck O'Neil and a player named Jackie Robinson. He went into great detail about the exploits of these and other Negro League stars and wondered aloud how they would fare against the major leaguers.

Yawkey, pale and weak as a kitten, was drenched in sweat and delirious. His face had turned fish-belly white. He had to fight several times to open his eyes, only to close them again each time. The black servant placed a cold cloth on his forehead and continued to talk of baseball feats that he had witnessed in places such as Mobile and Atlanta and Birmingham. He talked about Gibson's power and Satchel's speed. The words sounded distorted and otherworldly to Yawkey, as his fevered brain swam with ghoulish apparitions: ghostly ballplayers admonished him to change before it was too late. The Ghost of Seasons Past, an emaciated version of Babe Ruth, showed him graphic glimpses into the futility of Red Sox history and indicated the folly of continuing down the same path; the Ghost of Seasons Present, in the form of a snarling, profane Ted Williams, pointed his bat toward the obvious weaknesses on recent Boston teams. In the scene Williams revealed, all his Red Sox teammates appeared as Tiny Tim, hobbling from base to base on crutches—all but one. The other player, a cross between Jacob Marley and Pinky Higgins, tried to steal home, but weighed down by the chains of intolerance, he was thrown out by 10 feet. The opposing catcher, a demonic figure with white hair dressed entirely in white from head to toe, laughed derisively as he applied the tag. The image dissolved. Finally the Ghost of Seasons Yet to Come appeared before Yawkey. He was a black man and he appeared before a backdrop of vivid green ball fields where heroic deeds were being performed. He was wearing the immaculate home uniform of the Boston Red Sox. He said nothing but nodded at Yawkey and smiled knowingly.

The scene overwhelmed Yawkey's senses. At one point he sat upright and shouted, "It's time!" before collapsing once more onto the pillow.

Joe talked for a solid three hours before the doorbell announced the arrival of the country doctor. The doctor administered antivenin medicine to his wealthy client as Armstrong returned to other duties, all the while keeping a protective eye on Yawkey.

When the doctor left, Yawkey fell into a deep, dreamless sleep. In the morning, he awoke greatly improved and well on his way to recovery. He thanked Joe for his loyalty and his knowledge of snakebites and folk medicine. In a few days everything was back to normal and Yawkey returned to his regular regime of hunting and fishing, albeit with a healthier respect for the snakes of South Carolina. Although he was not yet ready or able to verbalize it, he thought he might have a better idea of what his Red Sox were lacking.

■ ■ ■

On April 13, 1945, two men were sitting in a small, airless room adjacent to the clubhouse at Fenway Park. The late afternoon sun sent a slender shaft of light through a narrow rectangle of window behind the cluttered office desk. The older man sitting behind the desk had a weathered face and rumpled gray hair and was wearing an ill-fitting but expensive brown suit. The younger man, jet-black hair slicked back, was intense and leaning forward.

"He looks real good to me," said the younger man. "Real good. He has good range, he makes all the plays, he has explosive speed, he can hit some, and he plays hard. He can lay down a bunt, and when was the last time we had someone who could do that? He can steal. I don't just mean outrun the catcher's throw, he knows how to steal a base. He reads the pitcher like a book. I saw him steal home twice in one game in Kansas City!"

The man behind the desk carefully unwrapped a cigar and examined it for a few moments in some detail before speaking.

"I've seen better. He's no Joe Cronin at the plate . . . not yet, anyway." He paused, making no move to light the cigar. "But he can play in the major leagues, no question about that."

The young man looked relieved. "Great! Should I draw up some kind of tentative agreement for him to sign? We can't wait around on this one. Rickey is not going to wait."

"Hold your horses, Sid!" said the older man irritably. "This is not just another prospect we're talking about here, you know. His ability to play the game is not the problem, as you are well aware. This requires some study. It would be the biggest thing to happen in baseball since they livened up the ball. We have to consider it very carefully, think it through. Is baseball ready? Is Boston ready, for chrissake? Am I ready?"

"If Boston isn't ready, then what city in the United States is ready?" The young man, scout and former Red Sox utility player Sid Lucknow, was in full stride, presenting his case. "Boston is the most liberal city in this country, isn't it? Harvard, MIT, BC, BU—universities on every corner. Muchnick isn't the only one who thinks it's time. We have a black population. We—"

"Negroes do not attend ballgames," interrupted Tom Yawkey, the owner of the Boston Red Sox. "They don't have the money and they don't have the interest."

"But if we get him, don't you think that'll change? Won't they come out to see one of their own?"

"I'm not sure I want it to change, Sid," replied Yawkey, looking directly at the eager young man for the first time. "I may have been born in the North, but I'm from the South and I think like a southerner. I grew up in a different world. What would those people—my people—back home in South Carolina think if I signed a Negro? Remember, it wouldn't stop with this one player, not by a long shot. If we sign him, be prepared to see the whole complexion of the game change. I don't know if I want to be responsible for that. I never denied that they could play the game. I've seen enough Negro League games to know what they can do. Just ask Dizzy Dean and some of those other major league barn-stormers about Buck Leonard or Josh Gibson or Satchel Paige. Ask Ted, he'll tell you about how they can hit. That's not the issue. Hell, they'd crucify him in Louisville."

"We could send him to the International League, to Toronto, or even ask Rickey to take him on loan in Montreal. Sort of hide him away and give him some experience with white crowds."

"You've given this a lot of thought, haven't you, you conniving son of a bitch?" Yawkey was grinning.

"Tom, can I speak frankly?"

"You always have, Sid. That's why you're my chief scout. I don't need any more yes-men around here."

"I think you have the guts and the smarts to do this thing. I think it will mark you as a pioneer in this game if you do. I know that you have your prejudices—hell, so do I. But I also know that beneath it all you're a fair man. I think you know that this is the smart thing to do and, more important, the right thing to do. Do it, Tom. Do it and they'll remember you forever. You have to think big to realize your dream of winning a World Series."

"Dreams. You don't have to tell *me* about dreams," said a suddenly thoughtful Yawkey. "Sometimes they are more powerful than any of us believes possible. . . ."

News of Robinson's signing hit the city of Boston with hurricane force. Details of the deal were splashed across the front pages of all eight Boston newspapers, along with black and white images of the seemingly exotic young recruit. There were photos of Jackie as a second lieutenant in the army, photos of him in his Kansas City Monarchs uniform, photos of him sliding into second base, photos of him in his UCLA graduation gown, photos of him as a Bruins running back, photos of him in the uniform of the Toronto Maple Leafs of the International League, his 1945 minor league team. Conjecture was rampant about how he would be received by Boston fans and players. Some columnists embraced his arrival; others were skeptical. Boston's liberal reputation was being severely tested.

Some writers, Colonel Dave Egan among them, questioned how Jackie would get along with the temperamental Ted Williams. The consensus seemed to be that sooner or later the two men would clash. The reasoning was that they differed so dramatically about their approach to the game, they wouldn't be able to tolerate each other. In fact, their baseball philosophies could not have been more different. One was a precise hitting scientist, the other a ball of spontaneity and energy.

The integrated 1946 Red Sox played together for the first time in spring training, and Red Sox veterans received Robinson the way they would any other rookie—with reserve, skepticism, and some resentment. The overriding sentiment seemed to be, how good can this guy be, playing in *that* league? Whose job is he going to take? Will he be too much of a distraction? Will he help us or hurt us? Some players went out of their way to make him feel comfortable; others studiously ignored him, stealing furtive glances only when he was taking batting and fielding practice. His skills in those departments seemed adequate but hardly extraordinary. Certainly he was no Ted Williams with the bat, no Doerr with the glove. And his arm was not strong, not by major league standards. And he was 28 years old! How could he possibly add anything to this talent-laden team?

The Sox began their spring schedule using Robinson sparingly. The proud son of a southern sharecropper had been added to the spring-training roster after a successful year with the minor league Toronto Maple Leafs. The plan had been to bring him to Florida for a taste of major league competition and then return him to Toronto for further seasoning. Robinson had other ideas. At first he started only occasionally and pinch hit or pinch ran. He filled in at third, second, first, shortstop, and the outfield and made himself indispensable. His arm was soon deemed too weak for outfield duty, and the Red Sox decided to play him primarily at shortstop or second base, with assignments at other positions as well. Fearing dissension in the tight-knit team, management insisted that he would be used "mostly as a backup" for veteran second-year second-sacker Bobby Doerr or shortstop Johnny Pesky. He suffered the usual rookie woes, facing previously unseen pitchers and learning about his teammates as he went. Nevertheless, he finished the preseason schedule with impressive offensive statistics, batting an even .310 and stealing 10 bases.

Robinson and Williams talked incessantly during spring training. Ted was at first intrigued and more than a little worried by the presence of the rookie. Race had nothing to do with it. The concept of base runners actually making things happen was foreign to the Red Sox way of doing things, and at first Jackie proved to be a distraction for the hitters, foremost among them one Theodore Samuel Williams. The accepted way—the Boston way—of doing things had been to get DiMaggio or Pesky, preferably both, on base and let the Big Guy drive them home. Base stealing was discouraged; the argument was that you didn't want to leave first base open with Ted coming to the plate.

There had been a few heated discussions between the Boston slugger and the newcomer. It had been a rocky start. Ted argued that Robinson had to be less active on the base paths. He found it a distraction, and Ted hated anything that jeopardized his focus. What could be more distracting than a base runner jumping around on the base paths trying to disturb the pitcher? Robinson was equally adamant. He was not about to change the strength of his game to suit anyone, not even this hot-hitting hotshot. They argued and they swore and they argued, and finally they arrived at a compromise. Above all else, both wanted to win ballgames, and Williams was smart enough to know that speed could be a vital component on a winning team. Jackie finally convinced him that his concentration was such that even an active base runner would not shake it, that the pitcher on the mound would be the one unsettled and agitated, giving Ted another advantage. Ted finally conceded that any negatives were outweighed by the positive of Jackie in motion on the bases. By the last game of spring training they were close friends and allies. Gradually, the two came to appreciate and respect each other's talents, and Ted began to see Jackie as a vital new cog in the Red Sox offensive machine.

On the field and in front of the press Ted had always quietly gone out of his way to ease Robinson's entry. He played catch with him during warm-ups and was vocal in his postgame praise of the multitalented shortstop.

The Red Sox shocked press and fans alike by announcing that Robinson would be going north with the team. Turning a potentially explosive situation to their advantage, they proclaimed that Robinson was so good that they could find no reason to return him to the minor leagues. They should scarcely have been shocked. He had already played with and against some of the best ballplayers in the country. Ticket sales that year got off to a brisker than usual start—everyone wanted to see the Red Sox back from the war, not to mention the new sensation. For his part, once in a Red Sox uniform, Jackie was determined not to return to the minor leagues.

Opening Day at Fenway Park is always an exciting event. Fans come out to see how the players have wintered and to check out the young hopefuls. They had welcomed some great ones over the past few years—brash young Ted Williams, quiet Bobby Doerr, scholarly Dom DiMaggio. But 1946 was like no other season before or since. The war was finally over and after three years of pseudo–major league ball, the Red Sox lineup once again featured some of the best ballplayers America had to offer. Just the presence of Ted Williams in left field and at the plate was enough to fill the ballpark and electrify the fans. But there was more. There was a buzz throughout Boston, in barbershops and bars in South Boston and Cambridge and the North Shore and all over, about a rookie ballplayer unlike any other the majors had ever seen. The newspapers had the Boston populace primed for the arrival of the rookie named Robinson.

For the first time in years, Fenway's opening game was sold out. Some fans in the capacity crowd were doubtless coming to see the Christian thrown to the lions, others to see an underdog David slay Goliath. Most had followed Robinson's exploits in spring training and, in best New England tradition, were reserving judgment until they saw him in action.

Significant pockets of black fans were also in attendance. Robinson's arrival at the ballpark had created a sensation, as fans jostled for a view of the unique rookie. They scrutinized him in batting practice, they examined his every move in infield practice, they watched him warming up with Ted Williams on the sideline, they observed his interplay with Boston players. No longer was Williams the sole focus of everyone's attention. The team now had two focal points.

The 1946 Boston Red Sox lineup was impressive to say the least. Johnny Pesky was made to order as a table setter for Williams. Bobby Doerr, among the best second basemen in the league, was also adept at reaching base. Ted's return from the service had excitement at a fever pitch. In his last season, 1942, he had won the Triple Crown and should have been named league MVP. The year before that, he had batted .406. Had the war years robbed him of his magic? The Fenway faithful could hardly wait to discover the answer. Dominic DiMaggio, the well-loved "Little Professor" with the scholarly spectacles, was back in center field. And veteran slugger Rudy York added punch at first base.

And then there was Jackie Robinson. Was he to be a significant part of this talented cast or strictly a sideshow? New England and all of America was about to find out.

The crowd roared their approval when the names of each Boston Red Sox player crackled from the ancient public address speakers. One by one, heroic in their spotless, white home uniforms, the players sprinted from the dugout and lined up along the first-base line. The loudest applause was reserved for returning hero Ted Williams, and he seemed in good spirits, kibitzing with teammates while swinging an imaginary bat. When Jackie Robinson was announced and ran onto the field to join his teammates, most in the crowd cheered loudly. There were a few scattered jeers but no overtly racist comments. Robinson went down the receiving line of Red Sox players and shook each hand. After the pregame ceremonies were finished and the national anthem had been sung with more patriotic fervor than usual, the players ran to their positions. Rudy York jogged to first base and Bobby Doerr to second. Johnny Pesky moved over to third base so Jackie could play shortstop. There was an audible buzz in the crowd as Robinson stretched and then took throws from his teammates. The rookie would be the starting shortstop for the Red Sox.

With Mel Parnell throwing hard, the top half of the first inning saw the Yankees go down in order on two ground balls to short and a line drive to Pesky at third.

To the surprise of the Fenway faithful, Jackie Robinson emerged from the dugout to hit in the leadoff position. He walked quickly from the dugout, vigorously swinging two bats above his head, tossing one to the batboy as he entered the batter's box.

Jackie took the first pitch, a strike on the inside corner. The second pitch was directly at his head, and he jerked out of the way just a split second before it would have made contact with his jaw. The fans, already on the edge of their seats, were now totally into the game. They shouted at the Yankees pitcher, and some questioned his ancestry. Robinson took a short walk from the plate to compose himself and dug back in again. Another pitch rocketed toward his upper body. Again Robinson ducked away, falling awkwardly in the dirt around home plate. The fans were now booing lustily. Robinson quickly got up, dusted himself off, and returned to the batter's box. With the count now 2–1, he knew that the pitcher would try to throw one on the outside part of the plate. He set himself nearer to the plate, defying the pitcher to throw inside. The pitch was as he expected, coming in low and away, and Jackie

> "Jackie was the greatest competitor I ever saw. He didn't win. He triumphed."
> —Ralph Branca,
> Dodgers pitcher, 1947

reached out and golfed it into right field for a single in his first major league plate appearance.

The fans stood and cheered this courageous at-bat. They were still cheering when Robinson ran on the very first pitch to Johnny Pesky. He slid into second base well ahead of the catcher's throw. This was not the way things usually happened at Fenway Park. The crowd continued to stand and cheer. The pitcher glanced behind him at the frenetic base runner and went into his windup. Again, Jackie was off at the release of the ball. Pesky swung protectively at the pitch and missed. The Yankees catcher, Aaron Robinson, caught the ball, sprang to his feet, and rifled it to third. But his throw was on the outside of the bag and Robinson's foot arrived a split second before the tag. Robinson was at third base with no one out in the Red Sox season opener. A shiver of anticipation ran through the ballpark unlike any that had been felt there in recent years. Usually reserved, cynical fans were chatting with their neighbors. With the pitcher rattled, Pesky drew a walk, and Ted Williams came to the plate to a standing ovation.

The catcher called time and walked to the mound to calm his shaky pitcher. They were obviously talking about Robinson and how best to defend against this radical base runner. The summit over, the catcher called for a fastball. Ted let the first offering go by as was his custom and creed—a strike on the outside part of the plate. He ground the bat handle in his huge hands as if trying to squeeze water from it. The next pitch was a ball, well outside Ted's precise hitting zone. On the release of each pitch Jackie danced down the line toward home plate, only to stop suddenly and return safely to third. The right-handed hurler could see him out of the corner of his eye. The catcher had to keep an eye on him too. Williams, uncharacteristically, stepped out of the box, as if he were ratcheting up his focus another notch as he'd taught himself to do in spring training.

The next pitch was inside and Williams turned on it and pulled it on a line over the wall in right field. The Red Sox had a 3–0 lead, and the new-style Boston Red Sox were born. The fans liked what they saw. So did the team. They were starting to warm up to this Robinson guy. Jackie and Pesky waited for the lumbering Williams to cross home plate, and when he did they shook his hand and followed him to the dugout, where the three were swallowed up by appreciative teammates. The lead was increased on a two-run Williams double and the home team won the game, 5–0. But the talk that night in Boston was not of Williams but of Robinson. They had seen Ted's magic before; this was something new.

The opening game had been a preview of things to come. Throughout the season, Jackie continued to play havoc with pitchers' concentration. Batting second, the unselfish Johnny Pesky was a master at hitting behind the runner, giving Jackie a chance to do his thing on the base paths. Williams would then come up with two ducks on the pond, and, invariably it seemed, at least one run would score. Opposing teams could not pitch around Ted because of the batters in front of and behind him. Bobby Doerr, Dom DiMaggio, and Rudy York gave no respite to opposing pitchers.

When the dust finally settled on the '46 campaign, Pesky led the AL in hits with 208 and rookie Robinson had finished second in the league in runs scored. Between them, Robinson and Pesky stole 41 bases (29 and 12 bases, respectively), and with strong hitters batting in front of him and behind him, Terrible Ted proved to be a one-man wrecking crew. He feasted on the pitchers' best offerings and gorged himself on their mistakes.

All was not rosy, however. Robinson received vicious hate mail and endured countless racist taunts from opposing players and fans, but he had his eyes on the prize and nothing was going to deter him. In Boston he had been quickly accepted by most of his teammates and by the vast majority of fans. When they looked at him they no longer saw just a black man, they saw a gifted ballplayer and a man who could lead the Red Sox from the baseball wilderness. It had been, after all, a very long 28 years since the Red Sox had last won the World Series. The liberal university crowd toasted his arrival, and the true blue-collar baseball fans of all persuasions saw him as a godsend. It seemed as if the only segment of the city that was really upset was that of the captains of industry and banking, who realized that they were going to have to open their businesses to qualified Americans regardless of color or creed. The country clubs could no

Jackie Robinson and Ted Williams demonstrated that baseball and brotherhood were more powerful in Boston than ignorance and hate.

longer exclude candidates who had fought for their country on the battlefields of Europe and were now being accepted on the field of play in our national pastime. Ted Williams went out of his way to be seen with Robinson on the field in every American League park, warming up before games, playing catch, or just talking in the dugout. Ted never said a word to the newspapermen he shunned, but it was obvious that he embraced the arrival of this seasoned rookie. Colonel Dave Egan, an outspoken advocate of the admission of blacks in baseball, noticed Ted's efforts, but for the time being he wrote nothing. Nevertheless, having a returning veteran of Ted's stature show him such support helped Jackie's cause immensely.

Ted and Jackie became fast friends. The West Coast Gang of Pesky, Doerr, DiMaggio, Williams, and Robinson were inseparable. They discussed the Negro Leagues at length, with Ted grilling the newcomer about Satchel Paige, Josh Gibson, and other legendary black players. They also discussed politics, and Ted and Jackie agreed that the Republican Party offered America its best chance for a bright future. Both were highly strung. One was spontaneous and unfettered in his reaction to criticism, the other, of necessity, was unresponsive and undemonstrative. Ted marveled at the self-control exhibited by his black teammate and attempted to emulate him. Ted, in turn, tutored Jackie on the most minute details of a pitcher's delivery and repertoire.

When Jackie got on base, which he did with amazing frequency, he transformed the Red Sox offense from a plodding, predictable one to a frenzied, dynamic, spontaneous one. Initially, the Red Sox used him selectively and avoided playing him in St. Louis and other "southern" cities. Eventually, however, he became the everyday shortstop.

The Red Sox clinched the pennant on Friday, September 13, 1946, as Ted Williams' inside-the-park homer provided Red Sox starter Tex Hughson the margin for his 1—0 shutout of the Cleveland Indians. Jackie ribbed Williams about his speed around the bases, and Ted agreed that it was less effort to hit them into the stands. Tickets for the World Series were gobbled up by victory-starved Bostonians within 48 hours of going on sale.

■ ■ ■

St. Louis, Missouri, October 15, 1946. It was the seventh and deciding game of the 1946 World Series between the Red Sox and the National League champion St. Louis Cardinals. The Cardinals had captured the National League flag by two games over the Brooklyn Dodgers. Some Cardinals players had balked at playing the Boston Red Sox because the Red Sox had a black player in their lineup. Two or three threatened to boycott the World Series itself unless Robinson was removed or at least benched for the duration of the Series. When National League president Ford Frick got wind of their scheme, he told them that if they did so there would be dire consequences, including a suspension from the league. "This is the United States of America," he said. "One person has as much right to play as another."

Some of the Cardinals and their manager directed racial taunts toward Robinson throughout the Series, but each taunt served only to make Jackie more determined to beat St. Louis. The abuse also succeeded in bringing the Red Sox together as a team.

The Series had been a seesaw affair from the outset. On the Red Sox side, Williams was mired in a horrendous hitting slump, the result of a nagging late-season injury. In Game 7, the Red Sox struck first, scoring a single run in the top of the first inning, but the Cards responded an inning later with a run of their own to knot the score. The Cards took the lead, 3–1, in the fifth inning and the outlook wasn't good for the Boston nine. But the Sox responded in the eighth frame as the Little Professor, Dom DiMaggio, came through with a double to drive in two runs and once again even the score, 3–3.

DiMaggio pulled a hamstring legging it to second and was replaced in center field by Leon Culberson.

Enos "Country" Slaughter of the Cardinals led off the home half of the inning and promptly delivered a single. The third Boston pitcher of the afternoon, Bob Klinger, mowed down the next two Cardinals batters, and it looked as if the Red Sox would strand Slaughter and get out of the inning with no further damage. But the Cardinals had other plans. Harry the "Hat" Walker came to the plate and promptly lined a drive over the shortstop into left-center field. Even before ball met bat Slaughter was off and running, approaching second when contact was made. Shortstop Jackie Robinson got ready for the relay from center fielder Culberson. The throw was not a good one, arching agonizingly slowly toward the waiting Robinson. Pesky shouted to Robinson, "Home! Home!" and when the ball finally arrived, Robinson knew that Slaughter was in full flight for home. He also knew that he didn't have the luxury of setting himself. In a single athletic move, he caught the ball at deep short, whirled in the air as if pivoting to complete a double-play relay, and completed a perfect strike to catcher Roy Partee. The sliding Slaughter was DOA, and the tie remained intact. It was a bang-bang play that silenced the St. Louis crowd and energized the entire Red Sox team. Johnny Pesky clapped Robinson on the back as they ran into the dugout. It was an ill-advised play by the Cardinals base runner, and he would be severely criticized for it for years to come. In fact, had it not been for this one play, Country Slaughter might have been a good candidate to eventually join Johnny Pesky in baseball's Hall of Fame.

In the top of the ninth inning, with the crowd still buzzing about the dramatic play at the plate, the Red Sox decided to go for broke. Jackie Robinson began the inning with a line drive single to left. He danced off first base, attempting to distract Cardinals pitcher Harry Breechen, who had been brought on in relief in the eighth. Racist comments were coming fast and furious from the St. Louis dugout and the stands, but this seemed only to inspire Robinson to become even more daring. His lead became so large that the pitcher could no longer ignore him. He threw once to first, twice, three times, four times. Even the St. Louis fans were becoming restive, and the Cardinals infield was positively squirming. Robinson had the pitcher and the whole Cardinals infield on edge.

Meanwhile, Johnny Pesky was at the plate, chuckling at all of the attention being paid to Robinson. The Red Sox bench signaled for the hit-and-run, and the left-handed-hitting Pesky executed the maneuver perfectly. Robinson was already moving at full speed when Pesky dumped the ball softly into right field, just over the head of Stan Musial, who was guarding the bag at first. Rounding second as the outfielder picked up the ball, Jackie arrived in a cloud of dust at third base, well ahead of the throw. Runners were now at first and third, with no one out, and Ted Williams was striding to the plate.

Ted almost invariably took the first pitch, especially when he was seeing the pitcher for the first time in a game. It was a subclause in one of his three golden rules of hitting: be patient. Since the National League pitchers were all new to him, it was a lead-pipe cinch that the eagle-eyed Teddy would take the first offering to get another look at Breechen's stuff. It just wasn't in his hitting DNA to do otherwise. The Cardinals scouts had watched him throughout the American League stretch drive and in the first six games of the Series, and if they were confident of anything, it was this. So far the scouting had paid huge dividends. Ted was by far the best hitter in baseball, but he was also in the worst slump of his brilliant career, suffering the effects of being hit by a pitch in a meaningless workout the week before the Series. His Series batting average was hovering around .220 on the strength of a paltry six hits. He desperately wanted to do something to help the team. He and Jackie had discussed this potential situation at length before Game 7. Jackie had explosive speed. Ted had unbelievable bat control. If the situation warranted it, they knew what to do. Both wanted more than anything to win.

Cardinals catcher Joe Garagiola signaled for a fastball. Breechen went into his windup and released the ball. To everyone's amazement, Ted Williams squared to bunt on the very first pitch, his second bunt in seven games. He executed it perfectly, pulling the ball down the first-base line as delicately as if it had been rolled there by the hand of God. At the moment the pitch left Breechen's hand, Jackie was on the move. He slid into home plate in a cloud of dust, just ahead of the flip from charging first baseman Stan Musial, who'd had to hold Pesky at first. The Red Sox now had a precious, if precarious, one-run lead. Ted stood on first with a wide grin on his face. He later admitted it was the biggest hit of his life. It had gone less than 60 feet. The Red Sox fans in the crowd cheered wildly, and Ted lifted his cap above his head to acknowledge their tribute.

The Cardinals got Doerr to hit into a double play, and Culberson flied out to end the inning. The Red Sox would carry their narrow margin to the bottom of the ninth against the potent Cardinals lineup. Tex Hughson, who they felt would be able to go one inning at the most, was brought on to close out the heart of St. Louis' batting order, but the Red Sox ace was almost out of gas. He gave up a triple to the first man he faced but then struck out the next two batters. Stan Musial, the National League's answer to Ted Williams, was approaching the plate. On the first pitch, Musial bunted the ball down the third-base line, a mirror image of the play a half-inning earlier. Without any hesitation, Johnny Pesky charged the ball, threw a perfect strike to home plate, and nailed the runner.

The Red Sox were world champions! Team members lifted Williams and Robinson and Pesky onto their shoulders, carrying them across the infield and into the Red Sox dugout. Back in Boston pandemonium erupted. Fans honked their car horns and poured from bars for impromptu celebrations.

The next day's newspapers were filled with stories of Robinson and Williams. The best headline came from the *Boston Examiner*, which proclaimed in three-inch type TED BUNTS! RED SOX ARE CHAMPIONS. A sour note was struck by Colonel Dave Egan, whose column began with a criticism of Williams' failure to tip his cap high enough. However, not even Egan could be totally negative on this day. He wrote an eloquent column about Ted's "low-key, but key nevertheless," role in making Jackie an accepted member of the Boston Red Sox. (From that point on, Egan and Williams ended their war of words, and when Egan finally retired his typewriter, Ted lobbied for his induction into the Hall of Fame.)

The city of Boston went wild. A ticker-tape parade attracted an estimated half-million people to downtown Boston. The loudest cheers of the day were reserved for the car that held Jackie Robinson and Ted Williams.

The team decided to have a lavish party to celebrate the victory. Various venues were considered for the event. Players wanted it to be an intimate but posh dinner dance, the victory ball. Just Red Sox owners, coaches, players, wives, and media representatives would be invited. But where to hold the gala evening? Pesky came forward to say that two weeks earlier he had rented the Imperial Ballroom of the Statler Hotel. Players and newspapermen appreciated the gesture and remember to this day the fact that Pesky held the ball.

Ted Williams and Jackie Robinson had combined their distinct individual talents to beat the odds and bring the world championship back to Boston. The team, the city, and the entire region would never be the same. Overnight, Robinson had become a Boston hero. He was asked to speak at Harvard and was presented with an honorary doctorate by Boston University. He and Ted were given twin keys to the city. The Red Sox quickly got a reputation as an organization that gave the black man a chance. Talented young black players across the country now dreamed of someday playing at Fenway Park, this haven of baseball tolerance and acceptance. Baseball caps with the distinctive "B" were worn by friends of freedom in every corner of the land, and the Red Sox's "Great Experiment" became a rallying point for the civil rights movement that followed. Historians would later say that this moment was one of the most significant in Boston and perhaps even American history.

In 1947 the Red Sox finished first again, five games ahead of the Detroit Tigers. The Red Sox defeated the Yankees in every meeting, knocking them out of pennant contention by early July. The previous two seasons had been both exhilarating and excruciating for rookie Jackie Robinson, a true baptism by the fires of intolerance. He had to endure racist taunts from opposition dugouts, beanballs and brush-back pitches, resentment from some teammates, and countless indignities that no man should have to face. Nevertheless, in 1947 Robinson batted .297 with 12 homers in 151 games. More important, he led the Red Sox with 29 stolen bases, finishing second in the AL to the St. Louis Browns' Bob Dillinger, who swiped 34. Robinson had been a spark plug all year long. Pretty soon the vicious bench jockeying all but disappeared; if anything, the taunts were having the opposite of their intended effect on Robinson.

Ted Williams captured the Triple Crown on the strength of 32 home runs, 114 RBIs, and a .343 batting average. The pattern was repeated over and over. Robinson and Pesky would get on base. Robinson would then rattle the opposing pitcher by jumping around on the base paths while Ted Williams feasted on fastballs like a hungry dog on a bone. The Red Sox won the World Series in four straight games over the talented but plodding Brooklyn Dodgers. If only the Dodgers had had a rallying force like Robinson . . .

By the start of the 1948 season, Williams and Robinson were accustomed to sharing the spotlight. Both had fiery dispositions; both were outspoken, intelligent, and articulate; both wanted to win. When the press got on Ted for some perceived shortcoming,

Jackie deflected the attention to himself with a statement about civil rights. When Jackie came under scrutiny for his outspoken views, Ted invariably popped off to the press. They were the perfect twosome, and the close friendship became even closer. They were an odd couple: Robinson was a graduate of UCLA; Ted was a high school graduate from Hoover High in San Diego with an insatiable curiosity and a probing mind. They talked hitting strategy, Williams being the acknowledged expert. They talked baserunning strategy, Robinson leading the way. To the delight of the rest of the team, they would needle each other endlessly. Ted called Jackie a banjo hitter and Robinson countered by suggesting that Ted lacked the necessary speed to play in the Negro Leagues. Ted had his prejudices—he hated pitchers and he didn't particularly care for singles hitters—but the man with legendary eyesight was colorblind.

The 1948 pennant race was one of the closest in American League history. Three teams—Cleveland, New York, and Philadelphia—battled through June and into the heat of July, when they were finally joined by the hard-charging Red Sox. Babe Ruth passed away on August 16, after a long battle with throat cancer, and the Red Sox dedicated the rest of their season to the greatest player in Red Sox history, the man who built the franchise and made the Boston Red Sox the most powerful team in baseball history. It was entirely fitting, since the Babe had led the Bosox to so many World Series and had provided the foundation on which Ted and Doerr and Robinson were adding new layers to the greatest dynasty in baseball history. By September 24, it was again a three-way race, with the Indians, Yanks, and Red Sox tied for first place. The Indians then won four straight and looked to be pulling away from the challengers, but the Red Sox won the last four games of the season, including two head-to-head battles with the hated Yankees, to finish in a dead heat with Cleveland after 154 games. The first playoff game in the history of baseball would decide the AL pennant. The Red Sox had won it all in '46 and '47, but that had only whetted their appetite for more postseason glory.

To try to hamper Williams' effectiveness as a pull hitter, the Boudreau Shift had been employed by the Indians and many other American League teams. The defensive alignment featured all Indians infielders and outfielders moving to the right side of the diamond. Over the past few years, Ted had adamantly refused to compensate for the shift, stubbornly insisting on hitting directly into the heart of this bizarre defensive alignment. However, in the 1948 playoff game, it was Jackie Robinson, not Ted Williams, who put a dramatic end to the strategy. Robinson used the strange defense to run wild on the base paths. In the first inning he singled, stole second on the first pitch to Pesky, stole third on the second pitch, and, after Pesky popped out, scored on a deep sacrifice fly by Williams. Ted and Jackie were greeted with enthusiastic slaps on the back as they returned to the Sox dugout. The same scenario was repeated the second time through the batting order, and the third. The next time Ted came to the plate, the Indians were in a traditional defensive posture. Ted promptly pulled a 498-foot home run into Fenway's right-field bleachers. The Red Sox won the game, 10–2, as surprise starter Mel Parnell limited the Tribe to just three hits. They were once again American League champs.

This Jackie and Teddy duo was proving to be unstoppable. There was an entirely new dimension to Ted's game, and it made him even more valuable to the Red Sox. The Red Sox had won their third consecutive pennant since Robinson joined the team. It was in every way a dream lineup. Robinson batted leadoff, followed by Pesky and Williams, then Doerr, DiMaggio, and Rudy York. It was Boston's version of Murderer's Row—with a touch of larceny courtesy of Mr. Robinson's base-stealing exploits. The Red Sox faced the crosstown Boston Braves in the Fall Classic and emerged with a 4–2 win in front of delirious Boston fans. Boston was quickly becoming the "baseball capital of America."

In 1949 the Red Sox won again, their fourth pennant in four years. They went on to win the World Series in five games against the Brooklyn Dodgers, surprise winners in the National League. The win added to the depression in New York, and fans no longer affectionately called them the "Bums," substituting a less polite term for that part of the human anatomy.

In 1951 the Red Sox added another black superstar to their already potent mix. He came to Boston because of Jackie Robinson. His name was Willie Mays and he could do it all. The Red Sox and Braves met once again in World Series play. The eyes of America were on Beantown as baseball hysteria gripped the nation. The two teams split the first six games and the Series came down to a dramatic seventh game. In the bottom of the ninth inning at Braves Field, the Red Sox held a seemingly insurmountable 4–1 lead. What happened next has become a shining moment in baseball history. The Braves scored in the ninth to pull within two runs. With two men on, Bobby Thompson, who had been traded to the Braves the previous year, came to the plate and launched an 0–1 pitch over the fence to win the game.

In 1952, the Say Hey Kid entered the United States Army and would be gone most of that season and all of 1953. The other Kid, Ted Williams, was also called back to active service, this time in Korea. Bobby Doerr retired after the '51 campaign and DiMaggio after the '52 season. With their lineup thus depleted by war and retirements, the Red Sox were unable to win in '52 and '53. But when Mays returned for the '54 opener, he took exclusive possession of Fenway's center-field real estate, and with Doerr's retirement, Jackie Robinson became the full-time second baseman, with Johnny Pesky moving back to shortstop. Willie Mays played center field like no one ever had. He ran the bases with the speed and abandon of Jackie Robinson, and he could hit—boy could he hit! And Ted Williams, back from military duty, could still play the left-field Wall at Fenway better than anyone ever had. This was a very different Red Sox team. Speed was now their trademark, and the burden for scoring runs was no longer solely on the shoulders of one man. The "Go-Go" Sox were a team no other could match, which was particularly frustrating for the New York Yankees, who were the last team in the major leagues to add a black player when they finally brought Elston Howard to the parent team in 1955.

■ ■ ■

During the precious few extraordinary seasons that Robinson, Mays, and Williams were to play side by side, the supporting cast changed, but the all-star combination of speed and hitting for average and power were a constant. No longer could opposing teams concentrate on just Ted Williams. The Red Sox were no longer content to just wait for the three-run homer or a two-run double. And no longer could teams pitch around Williams. With Mays now batting cleanup, pitchers were forced to pitch to Williams or risk even greater disaster if they put him on. With Robinson dancing around on the base paths, Johnny Pesky spraying the ball all over the park, and then Williams and Mays to contend with, the lineup was a genuine pitcher's nightmare. The Red Sox were a multidimensional team, an offensive juggernaut wielding a variety of weaponry.

Ted Williams, Willie Mays, and Jackie Robinson were the mainstays, but the Sox also had Billy Goodman, Vern Stephens, and Walt Dropo. Sammy White provided solid catching, and pitchers like Jack Kramer, Frank Sullivan, Tommy Brewer, Mickey McDermott, Mel Parnell, and Ellis Kinder toed the rubber.

The Robinson era was Boston's finest moment. It transformed a team and an entire city into a winner.

After the 1951 World Series, the Boston Braves' attendance slumped dramatically. There had even been rumblings in the media that the National League Braves might move their venerable franchise to some unnamed Midwestern city. Though many scoffed, Milwaukee was rumored to be a possible new "home of the Braves."

There was even some talk of putting a team all the way out on the West Coast, but no one gave that report much credibility. There was a public outcry at the very thought of moving the only club to field a team every season that professional ball had been played. The Braves had been representing Boston in the National League since 1871, and even though the Johnny-come-lately Red Sox, born in 1901, had become Boston's glamour team, the Braves hung on through those lean years, with the pitching duo of Warren Spahn and Johnny Sain holding them together. They had won the pennant in 1948 and 1951, but since then had fallen on hard times and fans were staying away in droves. In 1952, the Braves surprisingly bottomed out, finishing seventh. The franchise was in crisis mode. Should they move to another city and make a fresh start, or could they remain in Beantown and rebuild the franchise? Attendance grew somewhat with the arrival of Eddie Mathews, the home-run-hitting third baseman. The owners took a deep breath and decided to stay in Boston. The non-move paid off almost immediately. Suddenly the Braves had best pitching staff in the league, anchored by Spahn but also featuring Lew Burdette and rookie Bob Buhl.

With a full major league season under his belt, Eddie Mathews was now one of the most feared hitters in the game. Nevertheless, the Braves were drawing mostly friends and relatives to ancient Braves Field. And then along came another future Hall of Famer, Henry Aaron. Aaron, a soft-spoken outfielder from Mobile, Alabama, was a quiet, more efficient version of Willie Mays. With Jackie Robinson and Mays playing for the Red Sox and Aaron for the Braves, Boston fans had an embarrassment of riches. "Black gold," as one sportswriter put it. The two franchises drew capacity crowds to their respective ballparks and met twice a year in charity exhibitions. Many Braves and Red Sox players also met annually at the All-Star Game, representing their respective leagues and the city of Boston with pride. The All-Star contest was a showcase of the brightest stars in baseball, and with Willie, Ted, Hank, Eddie, and others, it was a genuine forum to establish league—and city—bragging rights.

"I had just turned 20, and Jackie [Robinson] told me the only way to be successful at anything was to go out and do it. He said baseball was a game you played every day, not once a week."
—Hank Aaron

"The pitcher has got only a ball. I've got a bat. So the percentage of weapons is in my favor, and I let the fellow with the ball do the fretting."
—Hank Aaron

By 1954, the Braves' revival had created the biggest rivalry in baseball—what became the perennial competition between the Boston Red Sox and Boston Braves, featuring Eddie Mathews, Johnny Logan, Del Crandall, Warren Spahn, and rookie sensation Hank Aaron. Aaron had come to Boston for two reasons: because of Jackie Robinson and because of his own hitting hero, Ted Williams.

The crosstown World Series was dubbed the Mays/Ted/Aaron Series, shortened to the MTA Series, and the entire transportation system was renamed in their honor. The one-mile stretch between Braves Field and Fenway Park was dubbed the Color Line, in honor of Jackie Robinson's single-handed transformation of baseball in America. And indeed, despite the fierce team rivalries, the personal rivalry among Aaron, Mays, and Robinson was full of mutual respect.

The interleague rivalry was embraced by the city of Boston, but each section of the city had its partisans. The Braves attracted the blue-collar crowd from Brighton, Allston, Cambridge, and Somerville, and the Red Sox were the darlings of the white-collar population as well as the university kids. Black fans came out in large numbers to see both teams, and many fans were simply enjoying some of the best baseball ever played, not so emotionally invested in which team eventually triumphed.

In 1954, Aaron and Mays were young players with their entire careers ahead of them. By baseball standards, the 28-year-old Robinson was old when he reached the major leagues. But in a few short years, he had revolutionized the game in the same manner that another Red Sox star, Babe Ruth, had once done. Babe did it with power, Jackie with speed, but the biggest difference was that Jackie also broke the color barrier. It now seemed that all of Boston embraced this breakthrough, taking renewed pride in a tradition harkening back to abolitionist days in the first half of the 19th century. The city was fundamentally changed by Robinson's presence. And Robinson was the spark plug. He ran, he slid, he was always on the move, a perpetual-motion machine upsetting rival pitchers and setting the table for Willie and Ted. The dimension of speed was something the Red Sox had always lacked, and now they had it and power. It was Ted Williams, Jackie Robinson, and Willie Mays against Joe Adcock, Eddie Mathews, and Hank Aaron. Warren Spahn versus Mel Parnell.

The Red Sox and Braves met in the World Series in 1954, 1955, 1956, 1957, and 1958. The Red Sox won in '54, '55, and '56 and the Braves in '57 and '58. During that time, Aaron versus Mays became the greatest rivalry of young players, and Mathews versus Williams was the classic rivalry of the sluggers. It was baseball at its dramatic best—"the streetcar series"—so called for the surface line up Commonwealth Avenue. Jackie received the nickname "the streetcar named desire" for the way he played the game.

Both franchises continued to have their loyal followers, both black and white. Sometimes the Braves came out on top; other times the Red Sox prevailed. But there was no doubt in anyone's mind that Boston, Massachusetts, was the city with the two best baseball teams in the world.

In New York the Brooklyn Dodgers were drawing small crowds; they finally moved to Milwaukee, where the city embraced them. The Giants, meanwhile, were lacking any charismatic players and became a Triple-A franchise of the Dodgers. The Yankees, with little or no chance of postseason play, instituted a best-of-seven series with the Triple-A Giants for New York City bragging rights. Cynical local fans dubbed it the "sub-par series."

■ ■ ■

Today the statue of Jackie Robinson stands next to those of Ted Williams, Babe Ruth, and Tom Yawkey in Monumental Park high atop the Green Monster at Fenway. Ted is in the middle of his classic swing, as is the Babe. But Tom Yawkey is watching Jackie Robinson, who is sliding into home plate, just ahead of the catcher's tag.

The social implications of Robinson's arrival on the city of Boston were even more profound than the on-field impact. As a ballplayer, Robinson set the tone for a racially enlightened American city and was in great demand on the lecture circuit. When the college-educated ballplayer retired after the 1956 season, he immediately entered politics. After a successful term on city council, he ran for mayor of Boston, following in Babe Ruth's footsteps. With Ted Williams stumping for him, he was elected in a landslide. He proved to be the best mayor the city ever had.

Thanks to Robinson, Boston became an oasis of racial tolerance and the symbol of a progressive and enlightened America. While in office, Robinson initiated a public works project that was the envy of every metropolitan center field in the country. Critics called it the Extravagant Excavation, but Robinson was undeterred. "If we don't do it now," he said, "our children are going to have a really big dig on their hands in the next century. I mean a really big dig. I foresee chaos and financial disaster if this is not done now." He also cleaned up Boston Harbor. "Hey, when it's no longer considered a miracle to walk on water, you know something has to be done," he explained. The Ted Williams Tunnel, the Willie Mays Overpass (also known as the Say Hey Highway), the Hank Aaron Airport, and the Jackie Robinson Bridge are all tributes to his vision and foresight. He and Ted Williams were strong voices for the Republican Party in Massachusetts and provided the first real competition for the strong Kennedy family, the Democratic cornerstone of New England politics.

After two terms as mayor, Robinson was courted by the Kennedys as a potential presidential running mate for Democratic candidate John F. Kennedy. As a staunch conservative, however, Robinson resisted these advances and instead entered Richard Nixon's political camp. He became Nixon's vice presidential running mate in 1960, and their Republican ticket defeated Kennedy-Johnson by a razor-thin margin.

President Nixon and Vice President Robinson faced many challenges, but Jackie provided the moral compass that the sometimes-tricky Dick Nixon needed to navigate safely through his first term. Nixon remained popular with the right wing, but his popularity with liberals and moderates began to plunge. In an attempt to bolster his popularity, he visited Cambridge, Massachusetts, the heart of liberal America, on November 22, 1963. As his motorcade proceeded along Massachusetts Avenue past Harvard University, where he was scheduled to speak to the graduating class of 1964, a shot rang out. Some say it came from Harvard's Widener Library, others insisted it was from the grassy knoll beyond Harvard Yard. Richard Nixon had been assassinated.

Nixon's motorcade; moments later, a shot rang out.

Jackie was quickly sworn in as president of the United States. To everyone's surprise, he chose Jack Kennedy as his new vice president, in an effort to unite the country. "Now I have two mates named Jackie," noted Kennedy. The Robinson-Kennedy administration made giant strides in civil rights legislation and was elected to two consecutive terms. Ted Williams was appointed as secretary of state. Thanks to Williams' diplomatic skills, at the end of their second term Cuba became the 51st state and former leader Fidel Castro subsequently joined a musical group later known as ZZ Top. When Robinson's two terms were completed, John F. Kennedy ran for the presidency and won, despite having just gone through a sensational divorce. He and new first lady Marilyn Monroe entertained lavishly at the White House.

Jackie and Jack: President Robinson and his vice president, John F. Kennedy. Robinson chose a Democrat as a means of uniting the government and the nation.

Chapter 6
Quotations of Chairman Lee: On the Media

"Always use kid gloves when handling the media; you don't know where they've been."
—Chairman Lee

"A ballplayer has two reputations, one with the other players and one with the fans. The first is based on ability. The second the newspapers give him."
—Johnny Evers

Whatever Happened to Colorful Players Like These?

Alex Johnson, then of the Cincinnati Reds, was considered a tough interview. A reporter once asked him, "Alex, you hit only two home runs all last season and this year you already have seven. What's the difference?" "Five," was Alex's reply.

Before the seventh game of the 1975 World Series, a reporter asked me how I would characterize the Series thus far. My answer: "Tied."

In an interview with George Bamberger, who was then the manager of the Milwaukee Brewers, a reporter asked about a triple play that had been pulled on the Brewers the day before. "It pretty much took us right out of the inning," Bamberger admitted.

> "He was definitely the player to be named later."
> —Rocky Bridges, commenting on Jose Gonzalez changing his name to Jose Uribe

Joaquin Andujar once explained to reporters: "That's why I don't talk. Because I talk too much."

With few exceptions, today's ballplayers and managers are so boring, predictable, politically correct, and cliché-ridden that their pre- and postgame interviews are scarcely worth a listen. Here is the way most interviews go. The ballplayer is Sammy Saccharine, pitcher for the Boston Red Sox:

Q: What are the Red Sox's chances this year?

A: We have to play them one at a time and give 110 percent, and with God on our side we can win.

Q: How tough are the Yankees?

A: I have nothing but complete and utter respect for that organization, from Mr. Steinbrenner down to the batboy— one of the top two or three batboys in the American League, by the way. They have the decided knack for attracting first-rate personnel.

Q: Do you get more "up" for Yankees–Red Sox games?

A: Not at all. Just another game to me. They all count the same in the win-loss column. The fans and media are the ones who make a big deal of it.

Q: Were you upset that the manager benched you for the past four games despite your 1.03 ERA?

A: Not at all. I needed to refocus.

Q: You are in a neck-and-neck race in the All-Star voting with the Yankees' Mickey Manson. How do you like your chances?

A: He's a great player and it is an honor just to be placed on the same ballot with him.

Q: Whom do you credit with your great year?

A: Almighty God. He is in our corner this year.

Q: Is this win the most important thing in your life thus far?

A: Yes.

Baseball is the only game wherein honesty is considered controversial and eccentric. Here is the way an *honest* interview with a ballplayer would go:

Q: What are the Red Sox's chances this season?

A: Once our shortstop gets out of drug rehab and our second baseman finishes his course in anger management, we expect to be vying for fourth place.

Q: How much effort are you willing to give to help the team?

A: Only 100 percent, Chuck. I know that puts me in a minority. Some of my teammates say they are giving 110 percent; I heard a few claim they are even giving 150 percent. But the most I'm willing to give is 100 percent.

Q: How tough are the Yankees?

A: They are the best team money can buy, that's how tough. Their first baseman has a higher annual income than Peru. I loathe George Steinbrenner and all he stands for.

"The players are too serious. They don't have any fun anymore. They come to camp with a financial advisor and they read the stock market page before the sports pages. They concern themselves with statistics rather than simply playing the game and enjoying it for what it is."

—Rocky Bridges

Q: Are the Yankees–Red Sox games more intense for you?

A: Intense? I hate those New York bastards with every fiber of my being. Before each game we get together as a team and stick pins in a Yankee doll. Then we burn George Steinbrenner in effigy and invoke the demons to rob him of his soul.

Q: Were you upset over being benched for four days, despite your low ERA?

A: ****ing right I was upset. That mother****ing son of a bitch manager is taking the food out of my kids' mouths.

Q: You are in a tight race for All-Star consideration with Mickey Manson. Can you beat him?

A: If those ***holes in New York don't stuff the ballot boxes, I might stand a chance. I'm twice the ballplayer that guy is. He couldn't carry my jock.

Q: Who do you credit with your team's success this year?

A: We're counting on Satan to carry us through, Chuck. God appears to be with the Yankees again this year.

Q: Is this win the most important thing in your life?

A: Well, the birth of my quintuplets was kind of special.

"You gotta be a man to play baseball for a living, but you gotta have a lot of little boy in you."

—Roy Campanella

Managers are equally boring:

Q: Why did you have Manny Ramirez bunting on a 3–0 count with two out in the ninth after Clemens had walked the bases loaded?

A: Manager's decision.

Q: Why did you take Pedro out in the ninth, one out away from a no-hitter and his 27th strikeout?

A: Manager's decision.

If I were manager, things would be different:

Q: Why did you take Pedro out in the ninth, one out away from a no-hitter and his 27th strikeout?

A: Excessive drug use on my part.

Q: Why did you put Daubach in to pinch run for Rickey Henderson?

A: Just a whim. Actually I have a side bet with Pesky that he'll get picked off.

The Press Conference

In keeping with my policy of openness and candor, I recently agreed to respond directly to questions from representatives of the proletariat. A hastily called press conference in an abandoned school bus outside Craftsbury, Vermont, resulted in the following exchange:

Q: Is the Green Monster really 310 feet from home plate?

A: All I know is, when I was pitching I used to scrape my knuckles on it, and Randy Johnson recently snagged his World Series ring on the manual scoreboard. I fear for Garciaparra's life if the Wall ever collapses while Nomar is going back for a short pop fly. He'd be crushed.

Q: What are your views on contraction?

A: If they are a few minutes apart, get her to the hospital. The universe is expanding, only baseball wants to contract.

Q: Are baseball owners too greedy?

A: It's all a matter of having fiends in high places. George Steinbrenner and Ted Turner both have satellites floating around up there. Soon they'll be trying to shoot each other down, like in *Star Wars*.

Q: Do you collect baseball memorabilia?

A: I don't keep anything that doesn't fit into the trunk of a '57 Chevy.

Q: Do you keep track of stats?

A: No. I know I beat the Yankees 12 times, but those aren't stats, those are memories that have been hardwired into my cerebrum.

Q: What is the difference between the Great Wall of China and the Green Monster?

A: One can be seen from space, the other is there because there wasn't enough space.

Q: Is the Green Monster considered aesthetically pleasing?

A: Frank Lloyd Wright would have approved of the Green Monster. He wanted to build within the natural guidelines of the earth. Everything corresponds to the area that you have available. It's a good use of space, follows the streets of Boston. It's amazing how much shit you can put in a small area.

Q: If the Red Sox retired Babe Ruth's number, would that remove the curse of the Bambino?

A: Sure. But he should also be elected to the Red Sox Hall of Fame. Put Ruth and me in together. We were both banished by the Red Sox. We can both go in posthumously, and we can go in face first so that they can kiss our asses.

Q: How slow were your pitches?

A: Dennis Eckersley called the stuff I threw "salad." He threw cheese and I threw salad. Mine was Caesar salad because I threw the softest but strongest stuff in baseball. I was like the Charmin of southpaws, the Mr. Whipple of pitching. If I were choosing a pitching staff, it would be made up of people who couldn't throw any harder than Omar Dahl. We'd probably bring in a couple of hard throwers just to break the monotony and to break in the catcher's glove.

Q: What will Don Zimmer be remembered for? ·

A: Hemorrhoids.

Q: Did you read his book, *Zim*?

A: No, I don't read fiction.

Q: You are a proponent of Zen. His nickname is Zim. Any connection?

A: Zen uses contemplation and solitary study to achieve discipline and self-enlightenment. Zimmer uses Preparation H.

Q: Again with the hemorrhoids?

A: Zimmer is a lovable guy, but he's dumb as a post. Anyone who would go out and sell hemorrhoid medication is asking for it. My advice to him would be to use bioflavones. I think we are interlinked, because ever since he's been doing those commercials my ass has been itching.

Q: In his book, Zim says that trading you to Montreal for Stan Papi was a good deal.

A: That's why he's still coaching. He put all his investment money into Edsel and Bingo.

Q: He also said that you were the only person from baseball that he wouldn't allow in his house.

A: That's devastating news! I've always enjoyed looking at furniture from the fifties.

Q: It seems you've been in Zimmer's doghouse for a long time.

A: Every manager has a doghouse, but Zimmer's doesn't have a door on it.

Q: What do you think of the spate of celebrity boxing matches involving people like Tonya Harding and Paula Jones?

A: There is no way I would get in the ring with Tonya Harding!

Q: I was thinking more of you versus Don Zimmer.

A: No. Why would I want to punch on the tar baby? Uncle Remus said, "Don't punch the tar baby, Brer Rabbit."

Q: Have you been blackballed by the Red Sox?

A: Yes. It began with the old regime, starting with Haywood Sullivan, Mrs. Yawkey, and Mr. Harrington. They are all from that period when I was let go. I think that the press has helped to keep it going because I'm always throwing things out—little vignettes. They keep reopening the wounds, picking the scabs. I do it just to keep sane in an insane world.

Q: What do you think of the new owners?

A: John Henry and I agree on the sanctity of Fenway Park, that we should try to do everything in our power to fix it. He and I are kindred spirits in that way. I am more of a traditionalist than any of the interim owners, from Mr. Yawkey to the present, have been. I think that John Henry has a little of Tom Yawkey in him. I think all the others considered it just a business. If you live long enough, people eventually come around to your way of thinking. A prophet in his time is not well respected.

Q: Who could do better in an ownership role?

A: I've often thought that the ideal Red Sox organization would have Stephen King as owner, me as general manager, Rod Dedeaux or Dick Williams as manager, and Laurie Cabot, the witch, as pitching coach. Luis Tiant would be my third-base coach, waving runners in with his huge Cuban cigar through a cloud of toxic smoke. I'd bring Bernie Carbo back every Sunday for the Bible meetings.

Q: Was baseball created by God, or did it evolve from the primordial ooze?

A: The Bible says it all started "in the big inning." So it was a creation thing, it has to be, although it didn't really get off the ground the first time. Adam was really bored and lonely, and he asked God, "What would it take to get a few guys down here so we could set up a baseball diamond and play a game?" God answered, "Well, that's going to take an arm and a leg," and Adam said, "Well, what can I get for a rib?"

Q: What is the effect of sex on a ballplayer's performance?

A: Personally, I would find the large crowds distracting. I have no lust in my heart, just four valves and an aorta coming out and a superior vena cava and some other items, but nothing I can't control.

Q: Did you ever run into Sam Malone?

A: No, Sam drank at the Bull and Finch. I drank at the Eliot Lounge.

Q: What do you think of Wally, the Red Sox mascot?

A: We've got to eradicate that guy. They should put a bounty on him and all the other rodents at Fenway Park.

Q: What did you learn about hitting from Ted Williams?

A: I learned that he was a lucky SOB to hit from the left side.

Q: When did you last see Ted?

A: The last time I saw Ted was in a baseball fantasy camp in Florida. He and I were just cutting up on the bench. He tried to put me on the spot with hitting questions, and I threw even tougher questions back at him. Ted loved it.

I had him rollin' and he took my fantasy team out that night for dinner. He got so mad at my theories, he threw a pu pu platter across the room and hit a wall.

I once told him that he was lucky that he hit from the left side because if he was a right-handed hitter, he'd have hit .225. I told him his dominant eye was his right eye. He said, "Whattaya mean, dominant eye?" That's when I pointed to a palm tree to illustrate my point. The last thing I remember is him driving away in a golf cart covering one of his eyes and looking at the palm tree.

Q: What did Yaz teach you?

A: Yaz taught me not to overbid in poker. It was a lesson that cost me all my meal money. He also taught me not to play pepper with him. Only rookies played pepper with Yaz, because he used to hit line shots off their knees.

Q: Who were the toughest right-handers you faced at Fenway?

A: Willie Horton, Frank Howard, Frank Robinson, Henry Aaron. I used to throw them soft stuff down and in and let them hit it off their own ankles. Then I made sure the paramedics were along the left-field line and then made them kill a few tourists with inside pitches. I'd get them 0-and-2 and then throw them slop away, get 'em out on their front foot.

Q: As a Zen Buddhist, can you reveal what is the sound of one hand clapping?

A: To hear this requires an enhanced level of consciousness. It is the sound made by the fans in Tampa Bay after a Devil Rays home run.

Q: If a tree falls in the forest and no one hears it, does it make a sound?

A: Let me answer your question with another question. If a Yankees infielder and a Yankees outfielder both fall out of a plane at the same time, which one hits the ground first? The answer is, who gives a shit?

Q: Are Yankees fans really all that bad?

A: Ferguson Jenkins, Joe Torre, and I were at an Old Timer's game at Yankee Stadium. Torre was our manager. He parked his car over in the South Bronx because he didn't want to have to sign autographs in the parking lot. Instead, he has this little alleyway where he parks his car. We sneaked out after the ballgame to get away from the press, and we went around a corner leading to this alleyway. All of a sudden we saw this naked broad dead on the sidewalk, just lying there. I took off my Red Sox cap and put it on her left breast, and Fergie took off his Texas Rangers cap and put it on her right breast. Torre took off his Yankees cap and put it between her legs. Then he took out his cell phone and called Apache, the police detachment for the South Bronx. They sent around a cruiser, and this plainclothes cop got out and looked over the scene. He lifted up the Red Sox cap, replaced it, and made some notes on his notepad. Then he picked up the Texas cap, replaced it, and made some more notes. Finally he picked up the Yanks cap, put it down, scratched his head, picked it up again, and wrote in his book. Torre said, "Officer, is there a problem here?" The cop replied, "I've been working this precinct for 18 years and that's the first time I've seen anything but an ***hole under a Yankees cap."

Q: That's an amazing story. . . . How did you fare against the Yankees?

A: I always pitched well against them. I had a visceral dislike for the Yankees organization. They were and are an elitist corporation with a media-hyped, self-promoted public image of cold arrogance that clashed with my philosophy.

Q: If, as you say, the earth is a baseball, what pitch is it?

A: A hanging slider. It's just waiting to be freakin' hammered. That's what I see right now.

Q: You once pitched for the Alaska Goldpanners and recorded an amazing ERA. How do you explain your success?

A: The farther north I go, the better stuff I have, because of the Coriolis effect. The closer I get to the equator, the worse I pitch. It's the same phenomenon that makes toilets flush and spin in opposite directions north and south of the equator. The earth's rotation causes a moving body to drift from its course—to the right north of the equator and to the left south of it. If I had played in Australia, I'd probably have a .200 winning percentage!

Q: If you are an anarchist, how do you organize the meetings?

A: Fair question! It's a meeting of one. I'm the only one who ever shows up. If nominated, I will not run. If elected, I will not serve.

Q: A Barbara Walters question: if the Boston Red Sox and the New York Yankees were nations, what nations would they be?

A: The Red Sox would be Albania—very repressive. The Yankees would be Nazi Germany.

Media Meditations

Of course, clichés are not the exclusive preserve of players. The media falls into that trap as well. All you have to do is tune in to any nationally televised Red Sox game from Fenway Park to hear them all. Whether it's Tim McCarver, Joe Morgan, Jon Miller, Chris Berman, or Bob Costas, the clichés are sprayed around like line drives off Wade Boggs' bat. Some of the perennials are:

> "God I hate Republicans!"
> —Chairman Lee

"Sure it's 16–3, but this is Fenway Park—and anything can happen."

"The Wall giveth and the Wall taketh away."

"The Red Sox are the slowest team in baseball."

"The Red Sox fans are the most knowledgeable in baseball."

"The Red Sox fans are the most cynical in baseball."

"Fenway is a lyrical bandbox."

> "I once called Boston a racist city and City Councilor Albert 'Dapper' O'Neil wrote me a letter, spelling several words incorrectly. I wrote back, saying: 'Dear sir: I feel I must inform you that some idiot has gotten possession of your stationery and is using it to say stupid things.'"
> —Chairman Lee

The Fenway Fateful

Even Red Sox fans are given to negative, cliché thinking:

"Sure we have a 12-game lead, but we'll choke."

"We may have won 10 games in a row, but the first loss signals disaster."

"Satchel Paige died the same year that my career in baseball ended. At that point, his spirit entered my body."

—Chairman Lee

"It shouldn't matter what race, what color, what religion, what nationality you are. That kind of thinking is obsolete in the 21st century."

—Chairman Lee

CHAPTER 7
Red Sox History Bites

Tony C Leads Red Sox to World Series Title

On one fateful day—August 18, 1967—Tony Conigliaro approached the plate and stood in against California Angels fastballer Jack Hamilton. Conigliaro had a habit of crowding the plate. Hamilton had a reputation as a brushback pitcher who protected his strike zone. It was an accident waiting to happen. Hamilton's first pitch caught Conigliaro on the side of the head. He fell to the ground like a sack of cement. After 18 grueling months of rehab, he returned to the Red Sox lineup in 1969 and managed to hit 20 home runs. In 1970, he hit 36 homers. It is difficult to comprehend the kind of courage it took to stand in against major league fastballs after such a traumatic event. He always had a blind spot that made his every at-bat terrifying.

In 1971 Tony C was traded to the California Angels, where he saw limited action and batted just .222. He was out of baseball from 1972 to 1974 and then made a courageous but unsuccessful comeback with the Red Sox in 1975. He played just eight seasons of major league baseball, but he was the fastest to ever reach 100 homers, and fans still wonder what might have been if not for the tragic events of 1967.

With a swing that was made for Fenway Park, the handsome right-handed hitter arrived in the major leagues with a bang. He hit a home run in his very first at-bat at Fenway Park, and all of New England embraced this hometown boy from Revere and East Boston, Massachusetts. He went on to hit 24 home runs in his rookie campaign while batting a lofty .290. In his sophomore year he led the American League in homers with 32, while driving in 82 runs. Another great year followed in '66 as he hit 28 more homers. And then it happened. In the midst of the most dramatic pennant race in baseball history, fate intervened and Tony Conigliaro's career was in shambles. The rest of his major league career was a battle against fear, and Tony C won that battle. Unfortunately, due to the damage inflicted by that errant fastball, he could not win the war.

On January 9, 1982, just two days after his 37th birthday, Tony Conigliaro had a massive coronary and lapsed into a coma. He died on February 4, 1990.

But what if . . .

The 1967 season was winding down to its dramatic conclusion. Carl Yastrzemski was tearing the league apart, each day finding a new way to win ballgames. And young Tony Conigliaro was just coming into his own as a hitter and a fan favorite. Since his arrival as a rookie in 1964, the handsome young hometown hero had captured the imagination of baseball fans across New England. This year he had continued his progress, and he was well on track for another 30-plus season. Under new manager Dick Williams, Conigliaro had some of the discipline and purpose that had been missing in the every-man-for-himself days of the early and mid-sixties. Blessed with a swing made for Fenway Park, the right-handed heartthrob was on the verge of stardom. Pitchers were beginning to pitch him inside, trying to move him off the plate. And he did crowd the plate, no question about that; he was courageous, perhaps to a fault.

Facing the California Angels, Tony C stood in against a tough pitcher by the name of Jack Hamilton. Hamilton threw hard and was particularly tough on right-handed batters. His first pitch was wide. The next pitch was high and way inside. Conigliaro instinctively snapped his head back, but the ball seemed to follow him, striking his batting helmet just above the bill before deflecting high into the air. A collective gasp went up from the sold-out crowd. Players gathered around the prostrate young man, and the Red Sox trainer rushed from the dugout. Seconds seemed like minutes. Conigliaro was not moving. Finally, after what seemed an eternity, he stirred slightly. A ripple of anticipation went through the crowd like a shiver. Conigliaro struggled to sit up, and when he succeeded, a roar went up from all corners of Fenway. The ball had missed his left eye by no more than two inches. Conigliaro refused help to the bench; he was determined to keep playing. The Red Sox manager attempted to remove him, but he persisted. He began to trot down to first base. After stepping on the base and hearing the roar from the crowd, he looked up and saw Jose Tartabull coming to pinch run. Conigliaro huddled with the first-base coach and Tartabull. Manager Dick Williams joined them. Finally, the manager and Tartabull trotted back to the dugout. Conigliaro was staying in the game. A discreet touch to his cap let the pitcher, the Angels, and the wildly cheering Fenway faithful know he was OK.

Hamilton was almost as shaken by the near tragedy as Conigliaro. His concentration destroyed, his next pitch was down the middle of the plate and Yastrzemski was all over it, hitting it on a line into the net above the Green Monster. The Red Sox went on to win the game and capture the American League pennant in one of the most exciting stretch drives of all time.

In the 1967 World Series, Conigliaro proved to be the difference as he homered in Game 7 against Cardinals ace Bob Gibson to give the Red Sox their first World Series title since 1918.

Along with Ted Williams and Carl Yastrzemski, Tony C went on to become one of the greatest hitters in Red Sox history. He finished his career in 1983 with 519 home runs, a .282 batting average, three World Series rings, and a permanent place in the hearts of Red Sox fans.

Game 7 of the 1975 World Series

It was Game 7 of the 1975 World Series between the Boston Red Sox and the Cincinnati Reds. Game 6, which had ended much earlier that same day, had arguably been the best baseball game ever played, ending dramatically with a Carlton Fisk home run in the bottom of the twelfth.

I, Williams Francis Lee, was chosen to make the biggest start of my colorful and, I have to say in all modesty, productive career. I was the pitcher for Game 7. I had originally been slated to start Game 6, but following three rain-induced postponements, manager Darrell Johnson opted to go with the now-rested Luis Tiant in that do-or-die matchup.

Now it was up to me to end 57 years of championship drought. Wednesday, October 22, 1975, broke fine and promising. All of New England—indeed all of the United States and other baseball-loving nations—was abuzz with talk of Game 6. Columnist Ray Fitzgerald suggested, only partly facetiously, that there should not be a seventh game, that everyone just walk away with the memory of the Ultimate Baseball Game to carry them through the winter. It was a nice thought, but baseball officials are not a sentimental or idealistic lot. Oh, if only we had listened to Ray, because Game 7 of the '75 Series was to become the biggest anticlimax in Red Sox history.

The Fenway faithful were still shaking themselves from the calm that followed the storm of Game 6. The fans could scarcely appreciate the tableau that was unfolding before them. I was pitching well, and we took an early 3–0 lead into the top of the sixth. And then the Big Red Machine kicked into gear. That annoying automaton Pete Rose singled, and I retired the always-dangerous Joe Morgan on a fly ball to right. Future Hall of Famer Johnny Bench then hit a routine ground ball to shortstop Rick the "Rooster" Burleson for what looked like a sure double play. The Rooster threw the ball to Denny Doyle at second for the force. With Rose bearing down on him, Doyle's throw to first went wide of Yaz and ended up in the Boston dugout. When the dust had cleared, Bench was on second base and Tony Perez, the Big Red RBI machine, was ambling to the plate.

Now, let me say something about the mentality that allowed the botched double play to happen. There's a whole psychology involved in the decision to move Doyle out of double-play position when you are ahead in the ballgame. By moving him off second, you're not playing aggressive defense. You're not taking the game *to them.* You're saying that they are going to hit the ball the other way, and I'm saying that I want my second baseman and shortstop close enough to second base so that if my pitch is effective and the ground ball is hit properly, we can get a double play—automatically. That's called aggressive defense, as opposed to passive defense. I was *very* upset with that passive defense. And that's the other thing. It was obvious that I was visibly upset at that point. Why didn't the pitching coach come out then, before a mistake was made, before I let my emotions get the best of me and cause me to make a bad pitch? I admit I was both rattled and annoyed at the misplay in the field and decided to throw Perez a slow curve, a variant of the eephus pitch. I had been very effective with Tony, throwing him that slow, arching curveball. It was a pitch that mimicked the St. Louis arch. I thought it would be a good idea to throw it to him again. Unfortunately, Tony and I thought alike, and he proceeded to hit the ball over the left-field screen and several other Boston landmarks. Our lead was cut to 3–2.

In the seventh inning I developed a blister on my left hand. I walked Ken Griffey and then was taken out. The fans gave me a nice ovation, but I hardly heard it. Roger Moret came on to pitch for me. With two men on, Moret faced Pete Rose, and Charlie Hustle came through with an RBI to knot the game at three. Jim Willoughby was brought in and quickly put down the Reds uprising and sailed through the end of the eighth unmolested.

And then it happened. For some reason known only to Babe Ruth's ghost and Darrell Johnson's shrink, the Red Sox manager made a move that in hindsight is difficult to comprehend. With two men out in the bottom of the eighth, he pulled Willoughby for pinch hitter Cecil Cooper. In fairness to Johnson, since there was no DH rule in this Series, it was a predictable move. Cooper promptly fouled out to end the inning.

With Willoughby now in the showers, Jim Burton was fingered to pitch the most important inning of the season, if not the post-1918 period. For the most part, Jim pitched well. He just had bad luck. Ken Griffey received a free pass. Cesar Geronimo moved him to second on a sacrifice bunt, and Dan Driessen's ground-out advanced him to third. Rose walked.

After Pete Rose walked, Joe Morgan, the smallest but most essential cog in the Big Red Machine, stepped to the plate and delivered an RBI single to center field. The magic of the night before was gone. That rabbit had left the hat for good when Ken Griffey's foot touched home plate. We lost the game, 4–3, and the Series, four games to three.

Within the confines of a single October day, the Red Sox and their fans had experienced the thrill of victory and the agony of defeat. We had experienced the best of times and the worst of times. We had been blessed and we had been damned. We had seen the mountaintop only to be pushed over the side.

But what if . . .

When I awoke on the morning of October 22, 1975, I knew in my heart that baseball history was about to be made. Like all of New England, I was still on a high from Game 6 the night before, probably the best baseball game of all time. I had wanted to start

Game 6 and have Luis start Game 7. He could have used that extra day's rest, and I was ready and able to go. But manager Darrell Johnson opted to go with Luis, and it worked out well.

In a very strange way, this was the second part of a night-night doubleheader, Game 6 having ended at 12:34 A.M. The sixth game got my adrenaline going, and I couldn't wait to go to the mound. I told myself not to be overanxious, to let the hitters be the anxious ones. I knew that I would never be able to over-power these guys, but I never doubted that I could outsmart them. The Cincinnati lineup was a pitcher's worst nightmare, and yet I had slept like a baby the night before. They had Johnny Bench and George Foster and Cesar Geronimo and Ken Griffey and Joe Morgan and Pete Rose and Dan Driessen and Darrel Chaney. I was facing Don Gullett of the Reds, and, prior to the game, Reds manager Sparky Anderson said, "Win or lose, after this game Gullett's going to the Hall of Fame." I replied that after this game, win or lose, I was going to the Eliot Lounge.

As it turned out, Gullet was in the showers by the end of the fifth inning and we were up 3–0. Even with the lead, I could sense the paranoia of the Red Sox fans, although in fairness to them, it

Bill Lee liked to hold court in the Eliot Lounge. Between sips of his Budweiser, he would explain the movement that his curveball must make in order to deceive opposing hitters. He lectured his attentive audience of Harvard students and revelers about Bernoulli's principle of lift. The science behind the pitched ball has always interested Lee. So has the history of the game. His aunt, Annabelle Lee, was a renowned ballplayer in the women's leagues of bygone days—"the best baseball player in the family," says Bill—and he has grown up with a healthy respect for the traditions and the nuances of the game.

isn't really paranoia if someone truly is out to get you. And all evidence since 1918 suggested that someone was definitely out to get the Red Sox! Leading off in the top of the sixth, Rose singled, but I got the next hitter to pop up. Then Mr. Bench came to the plate. Out of respect for his power, I pitched him low and away, and I was rewarded with an easy grounder to Burleson. Although the Rooster made a routine play and had plenty of time to complete the DP, Doyle was out of position at second, having been moved into the hole by the coaches. Burleson's throw arrived at second at the same time that Doyle and Rose did. Doyle's hurried relay went into the Red Sox dugout. There were now two outs, but Tony Perez was ambling toward the plate like Atlas, swirling 14 bats over his head and using the 15th as a toothpick.

At this point, the spirit of Cy Young came and rested on my left shoulder. He said: "I recorded 511 wins, surely you can get this one." Then the spirit of Babe Ruth appeared on my right shoulder, and the Babe said: "Kid, there's a bottle of Scotch waiting in the clubhouse if you win this one." They had a calming effect on me, and I looked in at Perez. I decided to tease him with a slow curve and sent a tantalizing blooper just outside the strike zone for ball one. Then I threw my version of a fastball under his chin for ball two. Then another slow curve, this time just scraping the outside of the plate for strike one. I threw another curve that broke over the center of the strike zone and froze Tony for a called strike two. The count was 2–2. Carlton Fisk came out to the mound to discuss what I should throw in this crucial situation. Carlton wanted a fastball on the inside part of the plate. I wanted to throw an old blooper curve that would have Perez jumping out of his spikes to hit. We argued. Next thing I knew we were exchanging blows. I felled Fisk with a roundhouse left to his lantern jaw. He got up and dropped me with a punch to the side of my head. I staggered to my feet and head-butted him. At this point the home-plate umpire and all his crew were trying to separate us. The Red Sox players were in a state of shock, stunned into inaction. The Cincinnati Reds were on the top steps of their dugout, jaws hanging around their navels.

Finally, order was restored. The umpires were at a loss as to what to do. Carlton and I were teammates, and they had never encountered anything quite like this. They huddled briefly and then asked Fisk and me if we wanted to continue. We both said yes at the same second and the umpires conferred again. The home-plate umpire then told Perez to return to the batter's box and yelled, "Play ball!" Fisk gave me a sign. I shook him off. He dropped another sign. I shook that off. He started to rise and come to the mound but changed his mind. He dropped another sign and I nodded. I went into my windup and released a slow change-up. The ball barely had enough momentum to keep it aloft. I could see Perez's eyes get big. The ball seemed to take a lifetime to reach the plate. My entire life flashed before my eyes. I remembered being in my mother's womb. I remembered my first date, my first kiss, my first drink. Perez's eyes continued to get bigger until he looked like one of those paintings of little kids that you used to find on the walls of cheap hotels. He was fairly twitching with anticipation. I could see the beads of sweat forming on his upper lip. Finally, the ball was nearing the plate. Perez began his swing. He lunged at the ball like Roseanne going for a hamburger. He was way out in front. The effort of his massive swing almost screwed him into the ground like Bugs Bunny in those old Looney Tunes. Strike three. Side retired.

Fisk and I hugged in the Boston dugout, and all ill will was forgotten. We were brothers again. We failed to score in the bottom of the sixth, and the score was still 3–0. In the top of the seventh a blister on my pitching hand broke. I couldn't grip the ball properly with this fickle finger of fate. I debated whether to take myself out of the game but decided against it. Ken Griffey was the batter.

Each pitch I threw had blood on it. I psyched myself into a Zen-like state and willed the blood-ball into Fisk's glove. I struck out the side on nine Rh-negative pitches and bounded into the dugout, having given the Red Sox a much-needed transfusion. Physically and emotionally drained from the confrontation with Fisk and the intensity of the game, I knew I was finished for the day.

In the bottom of the seventh we failed to score again, and Jim Willoughby came on in the top of the eighth. He pitched scoreless baseball the rest of the way, and we won the game, 3–0.

We were the World Series champions. I went to the Eliot Lounge.

Bucky ****ing Dent, or Bucky Gets Lucky

The 1978 season represents and encapsulates almost 60 seasons of Red Sox frustration and anguish. The season is, in fact, a microcosm of those 6 decades, because in six months the '78 Sox and their fans experienced dizzying heights and depths so low that they would give an oyster a bad case of the bends. And the season-ending playoff game with the Yankees was a microcosm within a microcosm.

The '78 Sox were the team of Fisk, Lynn, Rice, Yaz, Evans, Hobson, and Scott; an offensive juggernaut that scored runs in clumps, like touchdowns. Their pitching was equally impressive. Starters included Mike Torrez (newly acquired from the Yankees via free agency), Luis Tiant, Dennis Eckersley, Jim Wright, and me. Relief came in the persons of Bill Campbell and Bob Stanley; Stanley would go 15–2, mostly in long relief. Their defense was impeccable, with rifle-armed Gold Glover Dwight Evans in right field, graceful Gold Glover Freddie Lynn in center field, and seven-time Gold Glover Yaz in left. The infield was equally tight. George Scott, an eight-time Gold Glove winner, was at first base; local hero, defensive standout, and speedster Jerry Remy was at second; fiery, strong-armed Rick Burleson patrolled at short; and the sometimes-erratic but fearless Butch Hobson protected the hot corner. Perennial All-Star and team leader Fisk was a rock behind the plate and handled his pitchers like the assured veteran he had become. And leading the team into the AL pennant battle was Don Zimmer, a respected baseball man who had paid his dues as both a player and a coach. In short, the 1978 Sox were a team with no apparent weaknesses, a team with power, defense, and good pitching. Some were even bold enough to say this was a team of destiny.

As the season got under way, the Red Sox did not disappoint. In April they won eight in a row, claimed first place in mid-May, and by mid-June were an astonishing 43–19. They had captured the imagination not only of Boston, where they were 26–4, but also of every AL city. Over the course of the season, they out-drew even the Yankees (4,503,756 to 4,493,104) in combined home and road attendance. The Yankees under embattled Billy Martin, meanwhile, were struggling amidst the turmoil of a dressing room peopled by personalities such as Reggie and George and Graig and Sparky and Mickey and Lou. In head-to-head competition, the Red Sox had beaten their archenemies four times in six games before the All-Star break, and Boston all but seceded from the state of Massachusetts as the team entered a state of rapture. They won so often that the occasional loss seemed to matter not at all.

The Red Sox entered the second half of the season with a nine-game AL lead on the strength of a sterling 57–26 record and bright prospects for the remainder of the season. They continued to win, and they surpassed the 60-win plateau while recording only 28 losses. They were now 14½ games ahead of the *fourth-place* Yankees.

Then, quietly at first, the Yankees began to emerge from the weeds. Under newly appointed manager Bob Lemon, they went on a modest win streak of their own. They shot past Baltimore and Milwaukee into second place, a mere six-and-a-half games behind the once unreachable Sox. All of a sudden, injuries to Jerry Remy and Dwight Evans exposed weaknesses in the Red Sox bench, and Hobson, suffering from bone chips in his elbow, was a loose cannon at third.

Then, abruptly, the pitching went south too. Wright, Torrez, Tiant, and I all struggled to stop the slide. Riding the cushion they had established early in the season, the Red Sox still led the Yankees by four games entering the September stretch drive.

And then it happened. On September 7, the Yankees came to Boston for a crucial four-game series. What happened in those four days is still grimly muttered about in bars and taverns throughout New England and parts of Atlantic Canada. The Yankees shell-shocked Torrez in the series opener with a 15–3 score; in the second game the Bosox lost 13–2. Panic was setting in. In game three, a battle between aces Eckersley and Ron Guidry ended with Boston's ace in the hole, 7–0. Zimmer then bypassed me in favor of Bobby Sprowl in the series finale, and they lost again, 7–4. The Red Sox had been out-scored 42–9. The newspapers called it the Boston Massacre, but it was really much worse than that. In a massacre at least the enemy has the common decency to put the survivors out of their misery. The Yankees just invited them to New York—to their own battlefield—to continue the barrage. The Sox lost two more before rebounding to win the seventh confrontation behind Eckersley.

> "We shall heal our wounds, collect our dead, and continue fighting."
>
> —Mao Tse-tung

Just when it looked like the Red Sox were the '64 Philadelphia Phillies reincarnated, that they had choked down the stretch, the Red Sox began to win, and win, and win again. They won 12 of 14 in the face of overwhelming odds and intense scrutiny from Boston fans and media. Meanwhile, the Yankees became mortal again. Thus, the surging Sox and the yielding Yankees ended the season in a dead heat. The playoff game for all the marbles was to be played in Boston.

This was to be the death of the curse, the chance for the Red Sox to finally get the Babe off their backs, a retribution for 60 years of wandering in an arid World Series wilderness. The play-off game was only the second sudden-death contest in American League history. Interestingly, the other one also involved the Red Sox. In 1948, the AL pennant race had ended in a tie between the Cleveland Indians and the Boston Red Sox. That one was lost due to bad managerial choices and inferior pitching.

This time the Red Sox chose starter Mike Torrez, the former Yankee, to wreak sweet revenge on the worms from the Big Apple. What more fitting conclusion to the curse could there possibly be? The Yankees countered with their ace, Louisiana Lightning Ron Guidry, who would later be edged out for MVP honors by Red Sox strongman Jim Rice. The 1978 New York Yankees were the team of Reggie Jackson, Thurman Munson, Graig Nettles, Chris Chambliss, and Leapin' Lou Pinella. They were the perfect foil for the Red Sox. Munson and Fisk were fierce rivals; Reggie and Yaz were already bound for Cooperstown. They matched up as if cast by Abner Doubleday himself to take center stage in this decades-old diamond drama.

October 2, 1978, was a day that will live in infamy for the Boston Red Sox. At first things were looking good. The Red Sox staked Torrez to a 2–0 lead that held until the seventh inning, but then the Yankees' first two batters, Chambliss and Roy White, reached base on singles. Torrez got the next batter to fly out and Bucky Dent was up. Dent was a shortstop with a winning smile but very few offensive skills. He was to the term *Bronx Bomber* as John Rocker is to the term *humanitarian*. He was a good short-stop with Hollywood good looks and a will to win, but in the major leagues none of these attributes guaranteed success. Dent was batting .246 for the season, and even that average looked lofty compared to his .140 average over the last 20 games. The Red Sox had spun the wheel of fortune and had landed on the best possible person to face in this situation.

When Dent fouled the 0–1 pitch off his own foot, the situation could not have looked brighter for the Sox or darker for the Yanks; .246 hitters with sore feet who choke up on the bat are not threats to former 20-game winners. Indeed, Dent was almost comical, hopping around home plate on one foot as if trying to bring rain. The Red Sox players waited for him to resume his place in the batter's box, and for a while it was questionable whether he would be able to continue at all. When he did finally step gingerly into the box, it was with a new Louisville Slugger. He had cracked his bat on the previous pitch, and Mickey Rivers had taken one of his to the batboy to relay to Bucky. This is the same Mickey Rivers who, when teammate Reggie Jackson boasted of his 160 IQ, responded scornfully, "Out of what, a thousand?" So here was .246-hitting Bucky Dent, playing under an assumed name (he was born Russell Earl O'Dey), hobbled by a foul ball off his foot, and using someone else's bat, facing one of the better fastball pitchers in the AL. In his entire 12-year major league career, Dent would manage only 40 homers. Las Vegas oddsmakers would not have even bothered making book on his chances of going long.

But homer he did. With two men on base, he hit a lofty fly ball to left that looked as if it would be a wall scraper at worst and a fly-out to Carl Yastrzemski at best. When it cleared the Wall, all of Boston, all of New England and Canada's Maritime Provinces beyond, went numb. Fenway Park went as quiet as a tomb and much less cheery.

The Yankees were buoyed by the homer, and Reggie, perhaps shamed into action by the heroics of this pathetic pretender, chipped in with a homer of his own. The Yankees won the game and went on to win the World Series over the Los Angeles Dodgers. The suddenly not-so-unlikely hero Dent emerged as the MVP of the Series.

The Red Sox thus ended the '78 season with 99 wins. And unlike those lyrical "99 bottles of beer on the wall," it was a number that did not make the 26 long drives home pass any easier.

Certainly not Don Zimmer's. Even when he was driving to spring training in Florida the next April, some six months after the play-off game, his wife heard him muttering, "Bucky Dent . . . Bucky ****ing Dent!" The phrase became the Red Sox version of "Houston, we have a problem!"

Bucky Dent destroyed the Boston Red Sox in 1978. Buckminster Fuller, the inventor and architect, gave us all a blueprint to save the planet. His book, *Operating Manual for Spaceship Earth*, said it all. What the Red Sox needed was for Bucky Fuller to design a wall that would have prevented Bucky Dent's homer.

The 1978 season was the most tragic of seasons because we, the Red Sox, had everything. Our *number nine* hitter in the lineup had 30 home runs that year! You look at that lineup and it was rightly professed as the greatest Red Sox lineup of all time, the best offensive Red Sox team of all time. And we had Torrez, Eckersley, and me—the best pitching staff in the league going into the season. I remember a *Sports Illustrated* article from that year had all four of the starting pitchers with 10 wins before the first half of the season. We were 14 games up on the Yankees in late July. We had a great following. When we went to the West Coast we had more fans than the A's or the Angels. You have to realize that everyone came from New England originally, and New Englanders maintain their ties. We were America's team before the Atlanta Braves announced to the world that they were.

When Carbo was let go in '78 I protested vehemently. Bernie got traded because he didn't like to wear a cap because he had nice curly hair and didn't want to mess it up. We had survived the midnight trading deadline, so Bernie and I went out together that night. We gave each other a hug and said goodbye and congratulated each other on making it through another year. And then we found out that he was sold at 3:00 in the morning, which was still before the 12:00 deadline, Hawaii time. If the earth were flat, we'd still be together.

I went to Al Jackson before the playoff game and told him I wanted to pitch. I said, "My arm's healthy; I can prove to you that I'm back." I was ready to go. I'd worked hard in the bullpen the last month of the season, throwing every day, just honing myself down so that if the bell ever rang and I ever got the ball, I'd do my best job. I was ready to go! I went to him during batting practice and said, "I'll throw the ball over the new scoreboard onto Lansdowne Street to prove to you that my arm is perfect." And I did it. And he said, "That's impressive, but I don't think you're going to get in the ballgame."

Then I told him what was going to happen. At that point, the wind was blowing in from left field. I said that midway through the game the wind would blow out to left and he'd need a sinkerball pitcher for the last three innings. And he looked at me with that "Yeah, sure" look. Early in the game Reggie Jackson hit a ball that would have been out of the ballpark—it would have been farther out than Bucky Dent's—but the wind knocked it down and Yastrzemski made a great running catch in the left-field corner. Then we scored to go ahead 2–0. And then damned if the wind didn't change!

Bucky Dent fouled the ball off his ankle, apparently breaking his bat in the process. There was a long, long delay—I mean this was a five-minute at-bat—and supposedly he gets a bat—Wonderboy—from Mickey Rivers. Meanwhile, Torrez hadn't thrown for a while, and I guess he tried to throw a slider or a fastball that just didn't have anything on it and just hung. Dent hit the ball up into the wind, and just in that time frame the wind switched around. I mean the wind was blowing in when he fouled that ball off his ankle and the wind was blowing out when he hit the ball—just one pitch later!

Torrez threw great games down the stretch and he threw a lot of innings, but he was pitching on short rest. I was the freshest arm we had. If he had been taken out before Dent batted and I had come in and thrown a good sinker to Dent, low and away, he would have hit a ground ball back to me or to short or second and we'd be out of the inning. And we'd go on to win the American League and then go on to win the World Series.

A win against the Yankees would have thrown the yoke from the Denny Galehouse episode in the playoff game against Cleveland in 1948. We had never won a playoff game.

The Yankees had played very well to catch us, but it had taken a lot out of them. We had played well and won 9 out of 10 of the last games of the season to force the playoff. Rick Waits beat them in Cleveland or we wouldn't have even had a playoff. It was like the Fates were teasing us yet again. They could have put us out of our misery but they said, "No, we want to embarrass them one more time—at home—and have Yastrzemski pop up to end the ballgame."

(continued on next page)

And then Yaz's basswood relief would be in the Hall of Fame next to that La Montagne guy. He'd be depicted with his knee collapsed and overstriding and his back shoulder down for perpetuity. A hundred years from now when fans see a statue of Yaz, it'll be of him popping up. With Ted's statue, a thousand years from now fans will look at his statue and say, "Yup, looks like the greatest hitter who ever lived to me." And then they'll see Yaz and say, "Yeah, looks like a pop-up to me."

But what if . . .

May 9, 1961, 10-year-old adoptee Russell Earl O'Dey was practicing the piano. The weather outside was sunny and inviting. Wafting through the open window on the waves of warmish air, Russell could hear the faint, disjointed voices of his friends as they chose up for a game of baseball on the vacant lot next door to his Savannah, Georgia, home. Russell felt restless. He enjoyed the piano, but he also enjoyed baseball. And he played both very well. Small for his age, he nevertheless was a good fielder and a reliable hitter, but he had little or no power. Those same soft hands that marked him as a piano prodigy also made him the best defensive shortstop of his age-group in Savannah. Young Russell had two parallel dreams: to hit a pennant-winning home run in the major leagues and to win international acclaim as a pianist.

He left the keys and went to sit by the window. He watched the team selection play out according to the timeless rules of youth. Finally someone said, "Hey, where's Bucky?" They turned toward his house to see him looking back from the window. They shouted for him to join them. He paused and looked at the piano; then he looked back at the ball field. He appeared to be weighing something in his mind. After a long pause he shouted back, "Sorry guys, I'm trying to learn a piano piece for the school concert Friday night." With that he walked purposefully back to his piano and began to play, inexpertly but persistently. Through the window, his friends could hear the halting but recognizable chords of "Take Me Out to the Ball Game." They rolled their eyes at such a blatant waste of God-given baseball talent and returned to their game.

Seventeen years later, the Boston Red Sox and the New York Yankees met in the 163rd game of what the schedule makers had designed as a 162-game season. In actual fact, the Red Sox had already gone through three distinct seasons in the past six months. Season one was April to mid-August. They started as the hottest team in baseball, compiling a seemingly insurmountable first-half record of 47–26. Season two ran from mid-August to September 16 and featured something called the Boston Massacre. During this period, they swooned as dramatically as any jilted heroine of the silent screen, squandering a seven-and-a-half-game lead in no time flat. Before the dust had settled, the Yankees were three-and-a-half games in front. Season three was from September 17 to the end of the 162-game marathon. To their everlasting credit the Sox fought back and won every one of the last eight regular-season games to end in a dead heat with the Bronx Bombers. Now came season four, the cruelest season.

The single-game playoff was played at Fenway Park. In the seventh inning, the first two Yankees hitters reached base with the Red Sox still leading, 2–0. Shortstop Fred Stanley, a .219 hitter with one home run, came to the plate. For a moment it looked as if Yankees manager Bob Lemon would lift him for a pinch hitter, but Zimmer was thinking ahead. He walked to the mound, patted Torrez on the butt, and signaled right-handed sinkerball specialist Bob Stanley in from the bullpen. Stanley versus Stanley. Stanley's sinker was among the "heaviest" in baseball, and the Portland, Maine, native was at his best. On a 2–1 count, Stanley the pitcher threw his best sinker. The bottom fell out of the pitch as it crossed home plate, and Stanley the batter swung and popped the ball toward Red Sox shortstop Rick Burleson. Rooster gloved the ball on the second bounce and smoothly flipped it to Jerry Remy at second, who gunned it to Scott at first to complete the tailor-made double play. The inning over, the Red Sox still clung to a 2–0 lead. They were now six scant outs away from capturing the American League pennant in this roller-coaster-from-hell season.

The eighth and ninth innings would be a challenge. The always-pesky Mickey Rivers singled and stole second. Stanley, rattled by the presence of the hyperactive Rivers, threw Munson a fat pitch, and the surly catcher promptly singled to drive in the Yankees' first run of the game. It was 2–1, and after a hasty discussion with pitching coach Al Jackson, Zimmer ordered the bullpen into action. One right-handed pitcher and one southpaw quickly began warming up. The next batter grounded to short, and Burleson froze the runner before rifling the ball to first base for the second out of the inning. It was October 3 and up came the man they called Mr. October—Reggie Jackson.

As Reggie came to the plate, Zimmer strode to the mound once again and signaled for the lefty. At first, I didn't respond, thinking there must be some mistake. I was, after all, the man who publicly and repeatedly called Zimmer a gerbil. I was the man currently in the gerbil's doghouse. I was the man who helped to found the Buffalo Head Society, an organization apparently dedicated to making Zimmer's life a living hell.

I entered to a questioning buzz from the crowd, followed by recognition, applause, and the sound of 65,850 raised eyebrows. I had lost seven starts in a row at one point in the season and had thus earned my banishment to the bullpen. I was now being given a chance at re-entry into an atmosphere thick with tension.

On my first pitch, Reggie swung from his heels and pulled a screaming foul ball into the Boston dugout, scattering Red Sox players in all directions. He examined the bat, found it cracked, and walked toward the dugout. Mickey Rivers came to the top step and offered him his bat, but Reggie declined, saying: "Why would I take the bat of a .265 hitter with a 65 IQ?" My next offering was an inside slider. The batter turned on it, driving the ball high and deep but just to the right of Pesky's pole. Strike two.

I walked behind the mound and paused as thirty thousand fans took a collective breath. Two stinging fouls does not instill confidence in fans burned way too many times. I had thrown two inside fastballs and both had been crushed by Jackson, who would feast on fastballs like George Scott at the postgame buffet. I hesitated, having an internal argument with myself. My last post-season appearance had been in Game 7 of the 1975 series, when I unleashed a blooper pitch that the Cincinnati Reds' Tony Perez promptly blooped over the Green Monster. The Red

Facing Reggie Jackson, I would throw hard sinkers in on his hand, and he'd hit the first two balls off his toe. He'd be the guy lying there writhing in pain, not Bucky Dent. And then I'd throw him a sidearm slider low and away and his ass would come out and he would take it for called strike three and the game would be over. A hard sidearm slider! I pitched him that way when he was at the University of Arizona. He couldn't hit me with a paddle. He hated me. They all thought I was crazy and they thought, "He is going to hurt me." They thought I was going to bury it in their neck or their ear or something. Reggie always had that idea and so I'd pitch them hard in like that, and they would get on their heels and hit it foul. When they're on their heels, you thorn them a breaking ball away and they're toast. That's how you get Reggie out.

Sox went on to lose that game and the Series. I looked in for the sign from catcher Carlton Fisk. I shook him off once, twice, three times. Fisk then asked for time and trotted to the mound; his stiff gait was reminiscent of Frankenstein with arthritis setting in. We were arguing and Fisk was not a happy man. We could not have been more different in attitude and approach to the game. Fisk was a conservative, hard-nosed stolid New Englander with old-fashioned values and work ethic. I was a southern California liberal who appeared to go out of his way to create controversy and then glory in the spotlight. We had only one thing in common: we both loved baseball and we both had an unfettered will to win. Don Zimmer came to the top step of the dugout and glared toward the mound. He was about to come to the mound when Fisk and I came to a compromise, and Fisk ambled back behind the plate.

Would I throw the blooper again? Thirty thousand fans silently asked the question. Reggie Jackson, a historian of the game and an intelligent man who boasted an IQ of 160, also asked that question. This was, after all, the Spaceman, and you could never tell with me. I had brawled with the Yankees and called them Brown Shirts.

I went into my windup and released a sidearm slider that started for Jackson's letters, freezing him, and then broke across the plate low and away for a called third strike.

In the World Series that followed, the Red Sox played the Brooklyn Dodgers. The Dodgers outfield included Reggie Smith, a one-time center fielder in the fearsome Red Sox outfield of Yastrzemski-Smith-Conigliaro. Still numb from their playoff win, the Red Sox lost Game 1, 11–5, in Brooklyn on homers by Dusty Baker and Davey Lopes. Yaz responded with a home run, but it was too little too late. Game 2 was closer, but the Red Sox lost again, 4–3. The difference was a home run by Dodgers third baseman Ron Cey.

Back in Boston, the Red Sox hitters came to life, pounding 10 hits off Dodgers ace Don Sutton and relievers Lance Rautzhan and Charlie Hough. Leading the way for Boston were Carl Yastrzemski, Freddie Lynn, and Jim Rice.

Meanwhile, as the Red Sox organist John Kiley was playing "The Hallelujah Chorus," and Red Sox fans were cavorting around the bases with the players, somewhere in a Vienna opera house virtuoso pianist Russell Dent joined fellow musicians in a stirring rendition of a fugue from his idol Johann Sebastian Bach's "The Well-Tempered Clavier." Dent was so enamored of Bach's work that he was often referred to jokingly as Johann Jr. When he finished the piece with a flourish, Dent received a standing ovation for a performance that the music reviewer for the *International*

Bucky Dent, the famous virtuoso pianist, at his instrument.

Herald-Tribune called "more than just a hit. It was a home run in ivory." Dent's patron, Herr Brennerstein, was ecstatic. Of course there was inevitable grumbling from competing pianists, including one disgruntled German named Torrezstein who played in the wrong pitch. Torrezstein was managed by impresario Herr Don Zimmer-Frei. Zimmer-Frei hated the works of Bach as much as he despised Russell Dent. In a classic case of "pianist envy" he drove his Volkswagen back to the Rhineland uttering frustrated, disbelieving cries of "Bach und Dent . . . Bach und fugueing Dent!"

Game 6: Champagne Corks Pop in Boston

If ever there were a single game that represented, condensed, and crystallized all the trials, disappointments, and anguish of Red Sox fandom, it was Game 6 of the 1986 World Series. The Red Sox lost that game and eventually the Series, but the way they lost it was a sordid tale that would challenge the creativity of Charles Dickens and the cruelty of the Marquis de Sade. Even the names of the principal villains were positively Dickensian: Mookie Wilson and—for some unforgiving Red Sox fans—Billy Buck and Steamer Stanley.

> "I'm tired of it. I don't want to hear about it anymore."
> —Bill Buckner

> "I knew it was going to be a close play at first because the guy [Wilson] runs so well. The ball went skip, skip, skip and didn't come up. The ball missed my glove. I can't remember the last time I missed a ball like that, but I'll remember that one."
> —Bill Buckner, on Mookie Wilson's ground ball

The '86 Series between the Boston Red Sox and the New York Mets started in New York as Bruce Hurst and Calvin Schiraldi combined to shut out the National League champion, 1–0. Game 2 featured two aces, Mets fireballer Dwight Gooden against Red Sox franchise pitcher Roger Clemens. As it turned out, both aces were in the hole by the time the sixth inning was complete. The Red Sox accumulated 18 hits and easily defeated the Mets, 9–3, before a disheartened Shea Stadium crowd. They were returning to Boston up 2–0, and things could not have looked brighter.

Back in Boston, the Red Sox hit a speed bump when Bob Ojeda, a former Red Sox hurler, defeated Oil Can Boyd, 7–1. In the fourth contest, Al Nipper and the Red Sox lost to Ron Darling, and suddenly the series was tied 2–2.

> "I can especially empathize with Buckner because a couple of innings earlier I had made a very critical error. And I was sure that's the only thing I was going to be remembered for, for the rest of my life."
>
> —New York Met Ray Knight

Bruce Hurst then pitched brilliantly to hand Gooden his second loss of the Series, this time 4–2. The Sox had a 3–2 edge going back to New York.

Game 6 was played on October 25 at Shea Stadium in New York City. It was Roger Clemens against Bob Ojeda. At first things went swimmingly. Wade Boggs slapped a single off the usually reliable glove of third baseman Ray Knight, and it looked like it was Boston's night. With two outs, Rice doubled Boggs home and the Red Sox led 1–0. They scored another run in the second on the strength of consecutive singles by Spike Owen, Boggs, and Marty Barrett. Finally, ominously, Bill Buckner flied out with the bases loaded to end a game-breaking Red Sox threat.

Clemens was pitching brilliantly and did not give up a hit over the first four innings; however, in the fifth, the Mets broke Roger's spell on a walk to Darryl Strawberry, a stolen base, and a Ray Knight RBI single. Then Mookie Wilson singled and Dwight Evans bobbled the ball for an error. With runners on the corners, the Red Sox turned a double play but allowed the tying run to score. In the seventh, Roger McDowell came on for the Mets in relief of Ojeda. The Red Sox scored the go-ahead run on a Barrett walk, a Buckner ground-out, a throwing error by Knight that put runners on the corners, and an Evans ground-out.

With the Red Sox clinging to a tenuous 3–2 lead, Clemens closed down the Mets in the seventh frame. In the eighth the Red Sox had a glorious chance to add to their lead when Dave Henderson singled. But with a man on, manager John McNamara opted to pinch hit rookie Greenwell instead of veteran Don Baylor, who had 31 homers and 91 RBIs on the season. Greenwell struck out on three pitches in the dirt. Boggs and Barrett both drew walks to load the bases. Then, with two outs, the bases full, and the hobbled, .143-hitting Buckner due up, McNamara incredibly ignored Baylor *again,* and allowed Buckner to hit. He lined out to center to end the Sox threat.

Schiraldi was brought on in relief of Clemens, who had developed a blister on the middle finger of his pitching hand. The Mets quickly took advantage of the change, as Lee Mazzilli scored the tying run on a sacrifice by Gary Carter. It remained knotted, 3–3, after a scoreless ninth, and the game entered extra innings.

In the top of the tenth, Dave Henderson homered off Rick Aguilera to once again give the Red Sox the lead. After the next two batters were retired, Boggs doubled and Barrett singled him home for an insurance run. Corkscrews were poised all over New England.

In the bottom of the tenth, Schiraldi efficiently retired Wally Backman and Keith Hernandez. The message board flashed the words: CONGRATULATIONS RED SOX. Gary Carter was now all that stood between the Red Sox and a World Series championship. Carter singled. Kevin Mitchell was now all that stood between the Red Sox and a World Series championship. Mitchell singled. Ray Knight was now all that stood between the Red Sox and a World Series championship. Knight singled, making it 5–4.

Bob Stanley entered the game in relief of Schiraldi. Now Mookie Wilson was all that stood between the Red Sox and a world championship. Stanley brought the count to 2–2, and the

Red Sox were one out away. Stanley threw a wicked sinker down and away that eluded Rich Gedman's glove for a wild pitch. Mitchell scored and Knight took second on the play. It was 5–5. Everything else happened in slow motion. Mookie Wilson hit the tenth Stanley delivery toward first base. Buckner reached down for it, but it scooted between his legs untouched. The Mets won the game and two days later went on to win Game 7 and the World Series over the devastated, zombielike Red Sox.

But what if . . .

It was October 25, 1986, and the capacity crowd at Shea Stadium had gone through every possible human emotion. It was the bottom of the tenth inning of Game 6 of the '86 World Series. The large and vocal contingent of Red Sox fans who had possessed the courage to travel into the maw of the New York monster were on the edge of their seats. Their Boston Red Sox led the New York Mets by a score of 5–3.

The Red Sox had regained the lead in dramatic style in the top of the tenth on a homer by Henderson and an RBI single by Barrett. All across New England champagne was cooling. Fingernails littered the floors of living rooms and bars. The champagne corks were not yet popped because this was, after all, the Red Sox, and these were, after all, Red Sox fans. You took nothing for granted when you were a Red Sox fan. Massachusetts was and is much more of a "show me" state than Missouri will ever be.

Calvin Schiraldi, a Met the previous year, quickly dispatched Wally Backman and Keith Hernandez but then abruptly ran out of gas, allowing consecutive singles to Gary Carter, Kevin Mitchell, and Ray Knight. The bloop single by Knight, on an 0–2 pitch, sent Carter scampering home and McNamara marching to the mound. Bob "Steamer" Stanley entered the game.

It was at this juncture that an amazing thing happened. First baseman Bill Buckner, the epitome of the bloodied battlefield veteran, signaled the manager from the dugout. He motioned toward his legs and indicated that he was unable to continue. He limped from the game to the scattered applause from both the Mets' and the Red Sox's fans. On the bench, Don Baylor stared at the scene and said to Roger Clemens, "People may never know it, but that was the biggest move of Buckner's career." Dave Stapleton took over at first base.

Knowing that the tying run was a mere 90 feet away and the winning run was on second, Stanley decided to throw a fastball instead of his usual sinker. Completely surprised, Mookie Wilson grounded the pitch toward first base. The time between bat meeting ball and ball meeting glove seemed to pass in superslow motion for fans of both teams. In that split second, Babe Ruth left Boston for New York and Ted Williams went off to war twice. The speedy Wilson scrambled from the batter's box. Mitchell broke toward home, and Knight was well on his way to third. First baseman Dave Stapleton charged the ball, keeping his glove low, and the skimming grounder entered his glove at the precise moment that he stepped on the bag.

Red Sox players rushed from the dugout and mobbed pitcher Bob Stanley. Bill Buckner, the courageous first baseman, hobbled slightly behind the rest but was swept up with Rice and Lynn and raised into the air. Scattered but continuous applause came from the Shea Stadium crowd as the scoreboard flashed a gracious THE METS CONGRATULATE THE WORLD CHAMPION RED SOX. Disconsolate Mets players remained in their dugout looking out at the tableau as it unfolded. Some had their faces in their hands, others were staring vacantly at the celebrations of the field. The sizable contingent of Red Sox supporters went wild, rushing onto the field, where they were confronted by burly New York City police officers. The Red Sox were World Series champions! Not since the glory years of Babe Ruth and Ted Williams had the city of Boston had so much cause for celebration.

All over New England spontaneous celebrations began, and Jean Yawkey, doused with champagne in the visitors clubhouse, slurred her congratulations to Bob Stanley and Dave Stapleton.

During his fine 22-year major league career, Bill Buckner amassed 2,715 hits, while batting .289. He also won a National League batting championship and exceeded 100 RBIs on three different occasions. Despite all this, Buckner will always be associated with a routine ground ball that went through his legs in the biggest single disappointment in Red Sox history. To Red Sox Nation, the ball going through Buckner's legs is as historic as the first ship passing through the Panama Canal.

Likewise, relief pitcher Bob Stanley had a stellar 13-year career with the Red Sox during which the sinkerball specialist from Maine was a two-time All-Star. To many Boston fans, however, he is remembered only as the pitcher who threw the errant pitch that resulted in the New York Mets tying Game 6 of the 1986 World Series.

Clemens Stays in Boston!

Roger Clemens appeared to be the 6'4", 220-pound answer to Red Sox fans' prayers. The tall, tough Texan fireballer arrived in Boston in 1984 and, before leaving town 12 years later, he had twice fanned 20 batters in a single nine-inning game, had captured three Cy Young Awards, and was named AL MVP in 1986. He led the AL in wins in 1986 and 1987 and boasted the lowest ERA in the league in 1986 and 1990–1992. He also led the league in Ks in 1988, 1991, and 1996, his last season in Beantown. So why did he leave? And why is he so hated by New England fans?

Starting in 1993, Rocket Roger's career seemed to fizzle like a wet firecracker. He spent time on the DL and when he was able to pitch, his ERA ballooned to 4.46. After a brief revival during the strike-shortened 1994 campaign, he continued to struggle in 1995 and the first half of 1996. In the second half of 1996 he seemed to have recaptured his edge and his fastball, but it was too late. General manager Dan Duquette had lost confidence in Clemens and was intent on getting rid of him.

There were bitter battles in the press and his departure was acrimonious to say the least.

At the end of the season Clemens signed a four-year, $40-million deal with the Toronto Blue Jays. He left the Red Sox with 192 victories (tying Cy Young for the Red Sox team record), and team highs in strikeouts (2,590) and games started (382). But he also left Red Sox fans feeling betrayed. They felt that Roger had coasted for the past few years and had not given his all. They saw him as a mercenary who followed the money and had no loyalty to the city that embraced him.

Roger's move to Toronto and then to New York rejuvenated his career. He won three more Cy Young Awards (one with Toronto and two with the hated Yankees) and is still considered one of the best pitchers in the game. But in Boston the future Hall of Famer's name is spoken with a disdain usually reserved for Benedict Arnold and other notable traitors.

But what if . . .

Roger Clemens was not a happy man at the conclusion of the 1996 season. He'd finished the campaign with a losing record and had been booed by the Fenway faithful, vilified on a daily basis in the press. With trade rumors whirling about him, Roger's confidence was shaken. He sought out general manager Dan Duquette to air his feelings and discuss his future with the Red Sox.

Since the two men shared an appreciation for the finest in men's hairstyling, they met at a tony Newbury Street salon called Carbo's. Duquette wore a dark suit and a dark tie. Clemens wore sweat pants and an oversized shirt to cover his paunch. The two men had been sparring in the press for some time and this meeting would be of the "make or break" variety. When Roger first arrived in Boston, he could do no wrong with the press or the public. His talent was apparent for all to see, and both his desire to win and his work ethic were unassailable. Lately that seemed to have changed. Roger had put on weight and had had back-to-back seasons in which he underachieved. In fact, he was 40–39 over the previous four seasons. Was he washed up, was the Rocket's fuel spent? Many people, Duquette included, were starting to question his desire. When that happens, the next step is usually inevitable—a ticket out of town. And yet the Duke specialized in reclamation projects, pulling players off the scrap heap and giving them a fresh shot. Would there be some indicator that Clemens was salvageable? Duquette had made up his mind before the meeting to swallow his pride, try to put an end to their destructive feud, and see if he could ferret out some new thirst for thrust in Rocket Roger.

"Rog," he began. "Let's talk about careers. You've had a great one, but lately you've been coasting. It's too early for you to be in the twilight of your career. You don't like me. I know you don't, and that's OK. I grew up here in Massachusetts, and I want to win a World Series for the Red Sox more than anything in the world. Your contract is up. If you want to leave Boston for someplace closer to home, I can understand that. But the fans here really want to love you. They want the Rocket reborn. To me baseball is all about loyalty. I'd no sooner get rid of you than I would my only son. Why, I'd rather banish Johnny Pesky from the Red Sox dugout than see you leave us!" On hearing these words, a single tear welled in Clemens' eye and rolled slowly down his face.

Duquette continued. "Just this last month, you've not only thrown another 20-strikeout game but you've also moved into a dead tie with Cy Young for the most wins of any pitcher in a Red Sox uniform—192 wins! Wouldn't it be great to hit 200, and then 300, and maybe also win a couple more of those awards named after old Cy? You might not be young when it's over, but I'd love to see you in Cooperstown with a Red Sox cap on your head and a cluster of Cy Young Awards in your clutches."

Clemens shook himself from his reverie. He was stunned. Duquette's immense personal charm had warmed his heart and won him over. "Yes, that's what it's all about, Dan. You're absolutely right. I've always loved the fans here and I could never, ever turn my back on them. Move closer to home? I'd sooner take a job in another country! Canada or somewhere—play for the Blue Jays! Ha! No . . . no way, man! Boston's been good to me and to my family. I want to finish my career here and send all four of my "K" kids to Boston Kollege.

"Oh, sure, the Yankees could probably offer me big bucks. Steinbrenner's always tampering with me, flipping his checkbook open and shut. If I went the free-agent route, I could probably write my own check. Sure, I'd probably get in a World Series, maybe against the Mets, but with the pressure of playing in New York I'd probably do something stupid—like throwing a splintered bat at Mike Piazza. No thanks! I know you'll do right by me. All the players know you stick by your players through thick and thin. You'd be as likely to trade Mo Vaughn as me! Or—ha!—just let him go and get nothing in return!

"Face it, I haven't been that good these last four years. You know how I'm always reading? I remember reading how Ted Williams tore up his contract after the 1959 season because he'd had such a bad year that he demanded a 25 percent pay cut for having underperformed. Mo Vaughn's always telling me, 'It ain't about the money.' Well, doggone it, it's not! Send those Hendricks brothers a new contract for four more years and cut me 25 percent. What's good enough for Teddy Ballgame's good enough for me. If I win a Cy Young along the way, you can write a bonus check in my name to Mo's youth center in Boston. That's a good cause. I've got all the money I need, and then some. Use your money to get Pedro Martinez from Montreal. He's a real winner.

"And, Dan, I love you, man! Thanks for sticking with me. I'll come back and show you and everyone in Boston what I'm really made of. Why, I'll have six Cy Youngs before I'm through."

"Rog, you're the greatest," the Duke replied. "I have a feeling about next year. A really good feeling."

Quotations from Chairman Lee

"I've always maintained that the more egotistical and self-centered a ballplayer is, the better he's going to be. You take a team with 25 ***holes and I'll show you a pennant. I'll show you the New York Yankees."

"As a left-hander, my first good look at Fenway's Green Monster gave me a case of clinical depression. And that's when I saw it from the dugout. They should put Prozac in the water cooler when southpaws pitch at Fenway."

On Mark the "Bird" Fidrych, No. 20 of the Tigers: "We're on a first-number basis with each other. He calls me 3 and I call him 2."

On first seeing Fenway's Green Monster: "Do they leave it there during the game?"

"Winning is better than the next worse thing."

After the Red Sox blew six games against the Yankees late in the 1978 season: "Our pain isn't as bad as you might think. Dead people don't suffer."

"You have two hemispheres in your brain, a left and a right side. The left side controls the right side of your body and the right controls the left half. It's a fact. Therefore, left-handers are the only people in their right minds."

On relaxation technique: "I subscribe to the cosmic snowball theory. In a couple million years from now the sun is going to burn out and lose its gravitational pull. The earth will quickly become a giant snowball hurtling through space. When that happens, will it really matter what pitch I throw someone on a 3–1 count?"

"People are too hung up on winning. I can get off on a really good helmet throw."

Regarding an umpire's bad call: "If it had been me out there, I'd have bitten his ear off. I'd have Van Gogh'ed him."

(continued on next page)

"I was mad at Hank [Aaron] for deciding to play one more season. I threw him his last home run and thought I'd be remembered forever. Then he hit some more. I'd gladly have thrown him the last one."

"Kids don't learn the fundamentals of baseball at the games anymore."

"That was real baseball. We weren't playing for money. They gave us Mickey Mouse watches that ran backwards."

"You should enter a ballpark the way you enter a church."

As the two men left the salon, suitably shorn, the two hairdressers, Dirk and Lance, embraced and shed a tear or two. "That's what's been missing in this town," one of them said. "I've got a good feeling about our chances next year, too."

Bill Lee on Drugs

Authors' note: Please do not misconstrue this title. It is not intended to be a sensational, tabloid-style headline, only an announcement that what follows is Lee speaking his mind on drugs. No, wait a minute. Let's rephrase that. Bill isn't speaking his mind *while on* drugs, just speaking his mind *about* drugs. . . . Oh hell, you know what we mean.

"When they asked me about mandatory drug testing, I said, 'Well, I've tested them all but I don't think it should be mandatory.'"

—Chairman Lee

My name has long been associated with so-called recreational drugs. I have made some infamous statements on the subject, some of which received a great deal of media attention. My frankness about smoking marijuana earned me a rebuke from the commissioner of baseball. It also made me the cover boy for *High Times* magazine.

I was once asked if I preferred real grass or the artificial kind. My answer: "I've never smoked the fake stuff before." Nevertheless, I do not condone the use of performance-enhancing drugs. I want to watch the Boston Red Sox, not the Botox Bosox.

Drugs are no bigger a problem in baseball than they are in any other area of society. We are the canaries in the coal mine on that too. Drugs are no bigger than alcohol in daily life. The statement that excommunicated me from baseball is still true. When I was asked about drugs in baseball, I said, "Yes, they've been abusing nicotine, alcohol, and caffeine for way too long." And then they came down on me and said, "No, we mean marijuana." I said, "Oh, that. I've used that since 1968. I sprinkle it on my organic buckwheat pancakes. When I run my five miles to the ballpark, it makes me impervious to the bus fumes." That's when Bowie Kuhn took me off his Christmas list.

When I was with the Red Sox, whatever new drug they came out with, I was first in line to take it. Today the only thing that I am really high on is life. Baseball is my addiction. A good addiction. My performance as a pitcher at age 56 now depends on how many Advil I can take with my pancakes. Advil is a reprieve from death. That could be their slogan. Four of them at 200 milligrams each. Nolan Ryan does ads for them. I take them but I wouldn't do ads for them. I swear by them, though. They loosen up your lower back and add 10 miles per hour to your fastball. Suddenly you think you can run and you play really well—and then three hours later you go down in a heap and you're in agony again.

> "Something was definitely happening to me. My brain would start clicking into another dimension or time warp. It was as if everything was in 3-D, and I could visually grasp all three sides at once. Aside from that, I didn't get much of a buzz."
>
> —Chairman Lee, on his early experimentation with marijuana

Epilogue

As for Me . . .

Since leaving the major leagues—or more accurately, since the major leagues left me—I have lived a very full and varied life. The Red Sox traded me to Montreal after the 1978 season. In Montreal I was able to win two National League pennants and end the threat of Quebec separation from Canada once and for all.

I was elected to the Hall of Fame in Cooperstown in 1987, although my plaque is the only one with a bull's eye. I hope someday to be enshrined in the Red Sox Hall of Fame as well. So far, only their invocation of the rare "over our dead bodies" clause has kept me out.

After becoming a Nobel Prize laureate for my opus *The Wrong Stuff* (incidentally, *The Little Red [Sox] Book* will be my second such honor), I was persuaded to throw my hat into the political ring. I decided to start small and was soon elected governor of Vermont, but I was quickly appointed United States ambassador to China, where I was able to secure major breakthroughs with my now-famous "baseball diplomacy." I popularized the game of baseball throughout China and created a pipeline of players to Boston, where my good friend Bernie Carbo was the manager. At one point there were 15 players named Lee on the Red Sox roster, causing new clubhouse boy Don Zimmer to quit in disgust. The United States Senate began anticommunist hearings and immediately subpoenaed me to appear before them.

The hearings ended in chaos when I ratted on everyone I had ever met.

Riding my groundswell of popularity, I then ran for the presidency of the United States on the Rhinoceros Party ticket.

BILL "SPACEMAN" LEE

BOSTON RED SOX A.L. 1969-1978; MONTREAL EXPOS N.L. 1979-1982;
WON 119 GAMES AND LOST 90 FOR A .569 PERCENTAGE;
3.62 LIFETIME ERA; PERENNIAL ALL-STAR; WON NOBEL PRIZE
FOR "THE WRONG STUFF"; GOVERNOR OF VERMONT;
U.S. AMBASSADOR TO CHINA; PRESIDENT OF THE UNITED
STATES; MADE COVER OF "TIME," "NEWSWEEK," "ROLLING
STONE," AND "HIGH TIMES" ALL IN SAME WEEK; FORMER
OWNER, BOSTON RED SOX; BARNSTORMER; ICONOCLAST;
NAMED PLAYER OF THE MILLENIUM BY "MAD" MAGAZINE;
LOVER OF THE GAME OF BASEBALL; FRIEND TO THE EARTH.

The Spaceman lands in Cooperstown.

I convinced Dennis Eckersley to be my running mate and we were swept to victory over the first George Bush, with my campaign promise of "A chicken in every pot and some pot with every chicken." I won by a narrow margin, carrying every prison in the United States due to my vocal support of

> At a rally during Adlai Stevenson's unsuccessful 1956 presidential campaign, a woman in the crowd shouted, "Senator, you have the vote of every thinking person." Stevenson shouted back, "That's not enough, madam. We need a majority."

the early-release program, my so-called revolving door policy.

As president I legalized marijuana and hashish, but for personal reasons forbade the use of Brylcreem, except for medicinal purposes. Mark Fidrych replaced the eagle as our national bird, and Luis Tiant was appointed our ambassador to Cuba. I also changed the U.S. nickel to show a Buffalo head on both sides: Ferguson Jenkins and me. I signed the United States up for the Kyoto Accord to stop greenhouse emissions, and when the smog disappeared, the people of Pittsburgh and Cleveland were able to look around for the first time. Dozens of suicides were reported in both cities. I then unilaterally disarmed the country. We were immediately attacked and taken over by power-hungry Canadians and forced to live in roughly fashioned igloos while manufacturing hockey pucks under deplorable conditions. On a positive note, their beer was much better. As a geography major at USC, I should have known that 90 percent of all Canadians were massing along the U.S.-Canada border. I always thought they were huddling there for warmth, but now I realize they had colonial tendencies.

Despite the fact that the ensuing war of national liberation came to a successful conclusion, my popularity waned. Eventually I was caught misusing one of Luis Tiant's cigars in the White House, was impeached, and was driven from office. I then starred in my own religious program, *The Burning Bush*, on the Religion Channel, where I promoted my theory that George W. Bush is taking us all to hell. My new reality show, *Survivor*, about washed-up major league pitchers trying to make it on $400,000 in deferred income, has received critical and popular acclaim throughout the free world.

> "With the money I'm making I should be playing two positions."
>
> —Pete Rose

Following the lead of fellow politician John Glenn, I decided to enter the space program and give some validity to the nickname that has plagued me since my early years in Boston. At the express request of NASA, I then went into space to conduct experiments with dope. I was nine miles high by the time I realized that the dope they were talking about was Zimmer. We made the best of the awkward situation and became dear friends. He now says that, while I still can't enter his house, I now have permission to walk by it.

I later landed on the moon and uttered the now immortal words: "Hey, I can see my house from here."

For a short time I became a partner in a business that manufactured a line of baseball bats from Fenway's dismantled left-field Wall. The bats were called Green Monsters and were completely green in color. The bats popularized the expression "I really got good wall on the ball," and the phrase "wall to wall home run."

I was able to make enough money from the bat business to buy controlling interest in the Boston Red Sox. I immediately built a 62-foot rubber wall in left field to replace the old 37-foot wooden one. Line drives against the new Green Monster caromed quickly back to the infield, and power hitters were held to singles. The first year it was erected, right-handed pull hitters batted .125 with eight home runs at Fenway. Richard Simmons was hired as our fitness coach and quickly whipped the team into shape by "sweatin' to the oldies." After two seasons, I sold the team to an Arab sheik who is now lobbying President Bush to obtain oil-drilling rights in left field. His application is expected to be approved as soon as the president signs off on the Yellowstone Park clear-cutting and strip-mining excavation initiative.

Currently, I am holed up in a cave in the hills around Craftsbury, Vermont, where I am organizing a nonviolent militia whose purpose is the overthrow of government through a combination of noncompliance and apathy. Most of my recruits are indicted former CEOs of major U.S. corporations, in short the worst of the worst. We are possibly the best-dressed militia in America, however, and our expense accounts are the envy of every other militia in the area. In addition, we are able to obtain insider information at the drop of a hat. My financial lieutenant and part-time cook (thanks to the prison work program), Martha Stewart, and I are proposing to return the United States to the barter system. I am holding Bud Selig hostage and will release him only when baseball returns to its sanity. So far no one seems to realize that he's missing.

In 1998, the major leagues instituted a brand-new pitching award called the Bill Lee Trophy. It is presented annually to the major league pitcher who best combines the ability to induce ground balls with an ability to drink highballs.

I still manage to barnstorm and play baseball from Moose Jaw to Maine, although I now travel in disguise and carry a Canadian passport. My experiences on the barnstorming circuit have been unique to say the least. Once in Kedgwick, New Brunswick, Canada, a game was postponed in the fifth inning because the opposing pitcher had to go hear confession. Fisk used to hear mine right on the mound during games, usually with the winning run on third base and the count 3–2, but that was in the major leagues.

Universal Pictures is presently casting a movie version of my life. It will star either Mini Me or Danny DeVito as the prepubescent

> "[Baseball] is designed to break your heart. The game begins in the spring, when everything is new again, and it blossoms in the summer, filling the afternoons and evenings, and then as soon as the chill rains come, it stops and leaves you to face the fall alone."
>
> —A. Bartlett Giamatti,
> former commissioner of baseball

Billy Lee and Woody Harrelson or George Clooney as the troubled young-adult Lee. Billy Bob Thornton, George Carlin, and Charlton Heston are auditioning for the role of the older, mature me. Tom Yawkey will be portrayed either by Buddy Ebsen or Sean Connery, and Judi Dench or Madonna will be Mrs. Jean Yawkey. Bill Cosby will make a cameo appearance as Luis Tiant. Drew Carey, Don Rickles, Rodney Dangerfield, Anthony Hopkins, and Roseanne will portray Don Zimmer at various stages of his life (note: no gerbils will be harmed in the making of this movie), and Don Knotts, Jack Nicholson, or Jamie Farr will be Billy Martin. The role of Graig Nettles will be played by Billy Crystal or Mia Farrow. Mike Myers, reprising his role as Dr. Evil, will be convincing as George Steinbrenner. My various family members will be played by Gypsy Rose Lee, Bruce Lee, Christopher Lee, Vivian Leigh, Jamie Lee Curtis, Jennifer Jason Leigh, Lee Marvin, and Lee Merriwether. My son Spike Lee is directing, with a soundtrack by George Thorogood and Peggy Lee.

In a tribute to my career after the Yankee Stadium brawl, the movie will be called *A Farewell to Arm*, subtitled *Oh Fastball, Where Art Thou?*

Where Are They Now?

Following is an updated status report on some of my former Red Sox teammates and colleagues, as well as some noted opponents.

Bernie Carbo: A hairdresser and lay minister currently proselytizing and attempting to perform miracles in Theodore, Alabama, Carbo keeps trying to get dead dogs to rise up off the side of the road. But when he says "Heal!" they don't know whether to get up or sit down.

Carlton Fisk: Fisk was simultaneously enshrined in the Hall of Fame and embalmed in Madame Tussaud's Wax Museum. He's now a public speaker at an insomnia clinic.

Carl Yastrzemski: A perennial choice for the "worst dressed" list, Yaz is working on that fourth hair color called Just for Left Fielders.

Jim Rice: Jim is still working on his putting stroke. He drives the ball 340 yards and would be on the pro tour but, unfortunately, he putts that way too.

George Scott: Scott still coaches in Glens Falls, New York, and is trying to get back to the majors. He spends his weekends working as a United Nations interpreter.

Dwight Evans: Evans became a male model.

Rick Burleson: Rick started the Billy Martin School of Congeniality in California. It closed after violence broke out during an etiquette lesson.

Luis Tiant: The beloved Tiant is a purveyor of cigars and wisdom to the masses.

Dick Williams: Williams is still sticking it out in Fort Myers.

Don Zimmer: Zimmer spends his time as a part-time hemorrhoid ointment salesman and a full-time pain in the ass.

Graig Nettles: Nettles lives in Arizona, where he puts his quick hands to work milking pit vipers. The snakes are more afraid of his venom than he is of theirs.

Mickey Rivers: Old man Rivers just keeps rolling along.